The Theory of Comedy

ELDER OLSON

INDIANA UNIVERSITY PRESS

Bloomington *London*

To the memory of Muriel McKeon

Hacedme
un duelo de labores y esperanzas.
Sed bueno y no más, sed lo que he sido
entre vosotros: alma.
Vivid, la vida sigue . . .

Mr. Will Patten of Indianapolis (A.B., Indiana University, 1893) made, in 1931, a gift for the establishment of the Patten Foundation at his Alma Mater. Under the terms of this gift, which became available upon the death of Mr. Patten (May 3, 1936), there is to be chosen each year a Visiting Professor who is to be in residence several weeks during the year. The purpose of this prescription is to provide an opportunity for members and friends of the University to enjoy the privilege and advantage of personal acquaintance with the Visiting Professor.

The Visiting Professor for the Patten Foundation in 1965 was ELDER OLSON.

CONTENTS

The Theory of Comedy

CHAPTER I

The Problem of the Comic

We are about to embark on a theory of comedy, as the title
of this book suggests. I am old-fashioned enough to mean
comedy when I say comedy, and tragedy when I say tragedy;
by which I mean the dramatic forms designated by such
terms, and not forms which are narrative. And I do not want
to talk about the tragic sense of life or the comic sense of life.
It may be narrow of me, especially since it is so fashionable
now to do so, but I simply do not want to. I make this remark
in advance because when I published a book on tragedy a few
years ago, it greatly disappointed one reviewer because it was
indeed a book on tragedy—on the dramatic form, that is; and
this was apparently a dreadful thing for it to be. I should
have written about real tragedy instead—this, it seems, is life
itself—and I had talked about dramatic technique rather
than faced the true problems of the tragic sense of life and
the tragic vision and other tragic things of the sort. I am
sorry I missed the mark; but it happens that I was not aim-
ing at it.

If we are to discuss comedy, we must of course discuss the
comic; and I plan to do this in the present chapter. This
chapter will have two parts; a part in which I shall state the
views of everyone but myself on the matter, of course dis-
agreeing more or less with all of them, and a part in which I

shall state my own view, and try to make you agree with that.

The roads are very cluttered in criticism and scholarship nowadays; you have to clear the way before you can take a single step; and so, before we begin to theorize, we must take note of the fact that there are critics who are doubtful, either of the validity and usefulness of theory as a whole, or of its component parts: generalizations, definitions, and so on. L. C. Knights, for instance, states this view in his *Notes on Comedy*, published more than thirty years ago.[1] Professor Knights is particularly distrustful of explanations of comedy in terms of theories of laughter and social correction, but quite evidently his distrust extends to theory itself. Generalizations and formulae, he tells us, are mere "labour-saving" devices: "It is as easy and unprofitable to discuss the 'essence' of the tragic and comic modes as it is to conduct investigations in aesthetics which end with the discovery of Significant Form." Moreover, "no theory of comedy can explain the play; no theory of comedy will help us to read it more adequately."

L. J. Potts is fairly in accord with the former of these two statements, much as he would disagree with the latter:

I do not propose [says Professor Potts] to define comedy in so many words. It would not be possible to find any but a vague formula to fit *The Birds* of Aristophanes, *Tristram Shandy, A Midsummer Night's Dream,* and *Pride and Prejudice.* . . . Moreover, to give definition to an art-form is the business of the artist, and not of the critic; for the artist it is all-important to work within strict limits, but for his public and his critics it is equally important not to be tied to formulae. . . . Moreover, though definitions, like creeds, tell us a great deal about the people who make them, they are seldom completely valid for anyone else. In his famous definition of tragedy, Aristotle limits it to the drama, because in his day tragedy was the name of a branch of drama; it is no longer thus limited. He also ascribes to it a particular moral effect . . . but our ethical tradition is different from Aristotle's and it is not now generally true that tragedy *liberates* the mind of pity and fear. We all need to be able to make definitions, in order to clear our own heads and explain to other people what we mean by words of vague or variable meaning; but as the starting-point of discussion, they often hinder understanding more than they help it.[2]

I might multiply examples of this sort, but there would be little point in doing so. I also do not wish to try to refute the statements just cited. The only real refutation of the view that sound definition is impossible is the construction of a sound definition; the only real refutation of the view that a sound theory is impossible is the construction of a sound theory; and the only real refutation of the view that theory is unprofitable consists in the discovery of the evident benefit of theory.

Those who have agreed that theory *is* possible and valuable seem to have agreed on very little else. The critical literature of comedy is slight in comparison with that of tragedy, but it presents an equally bewildering variety of views. Perhaps the simplest way to deal with that variety is to divide it into three basic groups. The first of these deals with the problem of the comic, or the ridiculous, or the ludicrous (for the moment we will use these words synonymously) in terms of *what is laughed at;* the second in terms of *who does the laughing;* the third, in terms of some *relation* between the object of laughter and the subject who laughs. All of these are, of course, concerned with *why* we laugh; they differ in what they appeal to as the cause.

Plato, for example, belongs to the first group, if we take literally what he says in the *Philebus.* The ridiculous is a form of evil—the kind due to one's manifest self-ignorance with respect either to one's possessions or person or soul;

provided that one is weak and unable to retaliate when slighted, since otherwise he would be hateful and formidable.[3] (Aristotle's remark in *Poetics* 4 at least *sounds* very much like this, though we must discuss it another time: the ridiculous is "a species of the painlessly or harmlessly ugly or base.") Cicero, too, belongs here, along with the many later writers who adopted his doctrine of the ridiculous as a "certain baseness or deformity [*turpitudo et deformitas*] as defects in the characters of men not in universal esteem, nor in calamitous circumstances, nor . . . deserving to be dragged to punishment for their crimes."[4] Bergson, with his theory of laughter as arising from "the mechanical encrusted on the living," belongs here as well.[5]

The second group, who look for the cause of laughter in the one who laughs, find it in mind or body or both. We may restrict our discussion to the first of these. Hobbes, with his view of laughter as "sudden glory"—that is, sudden rejoicing in one's superiority to another;[6] Kant, with his view that it arises "from a strained expectation reduced suddenly to nothing";[7] Schopenhauer's "incongruity of sensuous and abstract knowledge";[8] Baudelaire, who sees laughter as stemming from a fault, not in the object of laughter, but in the one who laughs—indeed, it is for him a consequence of Original Sin and the Fall of Man;[9] Hazlitt, with his theory of a pleasant disappointment in trifles;[10] Freud, with his "economy of expenditure" and "suppressed infantilism"[11]—all of these belong here.

Finally, we have those who find the cause of laughter in some relation between the object of laughter and the laugher; thus, to cut the list short, Jean Paul Richter, who sees the ridiculous as founded upon the three ingredients of objective contrast, physical circumstance, and subjective contrast,[12] and Theodor Lipps, who sees it as an objective pre-

tense of greatness belied by a subjective realization of insignificance.[13]

I have just given very succinct statements of some very
complicated theories, and ordered them in an extremely
simple way, so that I am quite open, perhaps, to the charge
of oversimplifying them; and since I am about to be critical
of all of them, I may seem very unfair. But I must plead in
my own behalf that, except for some other succinct sche-
matism which might prove equally unfair or even more unfair, I have no alternative other than an extensive roll-call
of theorists, with an elaborate statement followed by an elaborate criticism of the views of each. This seems rather more
than we need, especially since the same results would ensue.
The fact is that we have no completely unexceptionable
theory of laughter, and this fact is very generally accepted.
Besides, I think we shall see that no one of these views is
really false; each is rather merely incomplete; and if we
succeed in constructing a complete theory, we may be able
to see the truth in each, as well as the particular place that
each occupies in a whole view. None of these theorists, it
should be said, goes so far as to deny that there is an object
of laughter, or a subject who laughs, or some sort of relation
between the two. The difficulty arises, in each case, from the
fact that a single kind of cause is stressed to the neglect of
other kinds of causes, and that even within the kind of cause
examined, investigation has not progressed to a degree of
adequate specification.

Thus all of those who analyze the object of laughter are
open to certain blanket objections: for example, that there
really exists in nature no such thing as the ridiculous, or, for
that matter, the serious; that one and the same object, viewed
in different lights, can cause quite different responses; that
laughter itself can proceed from infinitely heterogeneous ex-

ternal causes. These objections, indeed, tend to establish the contrary view, that the cause of laughter resides in the laugher, and not in what is laughed at. But this position is in turn open to certain blanket objections: for example, that we do not really consider everything as potentially ridiculous; that the view of things which supposedly constitutes the comic cannot be taken of everything and anything, and moreover does not always result in laughter; that some things do evoke laughter in most people; that laughter itself can proceed from infinitely heterogeneous internal causes. This drives us back to the first position, unless we take the third, viz., that the secret lies in some relation between the two— a matter I shall shortly consider.

For the moment, let us look at certain particular views. Plato's, for example; it is obvious that manifest self-ignorance, especially when coupled with weakness, may produce contempt, disappointment, annoyance, and a whole variety of responses other than laughter, depending upon the person responding; a rival might feel contempt, a parent disappointment, a stranger annoyance; indeed, most of us are far more frequently annoyed than amused by people of the sort described. The Ciceronian view of the ridiculous as baseness or deformity, even with his qualifications, is open to the same objections; so is the Bergsonian.

On the other hand, we may object particularly to the views at the other extreme. To Hobbes' theory of laughter as "sudden glory"; reflection on my superiority to an enemy in combat would produce relief, or joy, or confidence, not laughter; and so on, depending upon myself and the person to whom I suddenly find myself superior; conversely, it appears that laughter takes place without reflection on one's superiority. And Kant's theory of "a strained expectation reduced suddenly to nothing," Schopenhauer's of incongruity, and the rest; it is easy in each case to think of laughter not produced by the alleged cause, and of the alleged cause as producing effects quite different from laughter.

Possibly, then, the solution lies in a relation between the laughter and what is laughed at? Almost certainly, I should say, since the theories which treat them separately are plainly untenable, but not in the relations alleged by those who have taken this view. Consider Jean Paul's theory of the three ingredients of *objective contrast, physical circumstance*, and *subjective contrast*, in terms of one of his own examples. Sancho clings desperately all night long to the edge of a shallow ditch which he supposes a bottomless pit. This perfectly reasonable action, given Sancho's assumption, makes us laugh, according to Jean Paul, because we attribute to him a knowledge contrary to what he in fact possesses, a transfer we are induced to make through the physical clarity of the error. There are involved the contradiction between Sancho's efforts and the known circumstance (objective contrast), the circumstance itself, and the contradiction of both of these imposed by the attribution of our own view. This is very nice, but it does not work; the same formula precisely fits our witnessing of Oedipus' search for a guilty man, and underlies the tremendous horror we feel. Lipps' theory of an objective pretense of greatness contradicted by a subjective realization of insignificance is vulnerable in the same way; the formula fits many things other than the laughable. For example, disappointment.

Indeed, all of the terms expressing purely *logical* relations —such as "incongruity," "inappropriateness," "discrepancy," "contradiction," "paradox," and the like (and these may be found in all three kinds of positions we have been investigating)—are by themselves unsatisfactory. They are ambivalent, or rather multivalent, for they may be involved as much in

one emotion as another. My point is not that they are not involved here, but that of themselves they clearly cannot account for laughter, so that it is difficult to see why we should
think X ridiculous rather than Y. It is not the relation
merely, but *what* is related to *what*, that would seem to make
all the difference. A child wearing a man's hat is an instance
of incongruity, and may amuse us. But the children in William Golding's *Lord of the Flies* also supply instances of
the same incongruity between the childish and the adult,
and horrify us. For that matter, one and the same incongruity
—say, the child with the hat—may amuse you or horrify you,
depending on the circumstances, and your view of the matter. Indeed, the universe is full of incongruities, and if this
theory were true, we should never stop laughing.

No, I must say, unless we have been grossly unjust in
stating them, none of these theories will do. What, then,
will do?

Before we can attack this question, it will be well to do a
little ground-clearing. Let us begin with the matter of laughter. Laughter is not a single emotion; indeed, it is not an
emotion at all. It is rather, as Spinoza says, a physical affection of a certain kind; and it can proceed from all sorts of
causes, most of which do not concern us: for instance, from
external physical stimuli, such as tickling; from certain sub-
stances, noxious and otherwise, such as nitrous oxide, bella-
donna, atropine, amphetamines, and alcohol; from certain
morbid physical conditions, such as encephalitis; from causes
of a psychical order, such as hysteria or madness; from a desire to dissimulate embarrassment, or to seem jovial, and so
on; from contempt or malice and similarly unpleasant emotions, or the wish to signify these; from pleasure, mirth, and
joy, or the anticipation of these, as well as sympathetic re-
actions to them. It is clear, then, that even when not simu-

lated, laughter is only a symptom, and not a very reliable one, for it indicates contrary conditions; even when we eliminate laughter produced by physical causes, it is indicative not of determinate emotion but only of an excessive degree of some emotion. The human body tends to cathart any excessive emotion by certain physical outlets, such as laughter and weeping. Since these outlets are few, and the emotions many, an ambiguity ensues which parallels that of verbal ambiguity when a single word may represent many distinct, and sometimes even contrary, things. Thus weeping, for instance, can betoken extreme joy as well as extreme grief, as we all know, or can find out by watching the next Miss Universe when she wins the contest; and laughter presents the same ambiguity.

Obviously, then, we can dismiss laughter as a physical effect from our discussion; it is only an unreliable external sign of a particular *internal*—I mean *psychic*—phenomenon which is our real concern. The identification of laughter with this phenomenon stems only from our tendency to associate an effect with its most frequent cause.

I do not wish to call this phenomenon—*as yet*, at least—by any particular name such as joy, mirth, delight, or anything of the sort; all of these words carry connotations which may confuse discussion. Suppose, so to speak, we sterilize our phenomenon of verbal connotations by calling it simply the laughter emotion; and if you have any connotations with this term, please forget them. This emotion immediately lodges us in certain problems. Can a theory of it be constructed which will be valid for any object as well as for any subject who responds, whether an Einstein or a caveman, a noble soul or a villain? The answer is that *we can, if we can state the conditions upon which it comes to be.* Now it is obvious that it occurs only under certain specific conditions, otherwise we should all always be feeling it. We may note that it is a pleasurable feeling; that it is apparently a distinctively human feeling—at least we have no conclusive evidence that other animals feel it; that it is apparently natural to man, and—if indeed exclusively human—must be bound up with certain distinctively and exclusively human faculties. Moreover, it occurs *only upon a concurrence of three factors*, each of which may be said to be a cause, although in a different sense. These three factors are (1) a certain *kind of object*, (2) a certain *frame of mind* in us, (3) the *grounds* on which we feel. Thus we do not feel this emotion with respect to anyone and everyone, just as we do not fear anyone and everyone; and we do not feel it in every frame of mind, just as we do not fear in every frame of mind; and we do not feel it on every ground any more than we fear on every ground, but on certain grounds only. Clearly, then, we must identify the emotion by tracing along these three lines of differentiation; and here at once we see the difficulty of earlier theories, for each of the theorists we examined seems to have followed one only, or at most two, and in most instances even that was not pushed far enough. The result was that each could be refuted simply by pointing to variations within the uninvestigated areas.

The ridiculous has always been considered one of the objects of the emotion with which we are concerned, as its name implies; perhaps we can learn something about its nature by considering what happens when we ridicule someone. Ridicule is a particular kind of *depreciation*. We cannot ridicule someone by showing that he is extremely *good*, or *better* than most, or *even ordinary;* we must show that he is *inferior*, either to the ordinary, or at least inferior to what has been thought or claimed about him, by himself or others. But we do not ridicule someone simply by showing that he is bad; for example, that the pretended saint is in fact a mass-murderer, or that the mass-murderer is really only the murderer of a few, for he would even then be the object of serious concern. And we cannot ridicule simply by showing that he is not the object of serious concern; we must exhibit the *sheer absurdity of taking him seriously at all;* in other words, we must establish not the contradictory of the serious but the *contrary* of it.

Evidently, then, the ridiculous always involves a double contrariety: a contrariety to the good, and a contrariety to the serious. Like praise and blame, it is the product of a double value-judgment; for when we praise someone, we say that he has a certain quality which is both good and importantly so. It may appear that I have here fallen into the logical formulae of which I complained earlier; but please observe that these are *concrete* formulae: that is, they contain *matter* as well as *form;* it makes all the difference whether we say "contrariety" or contrariety *to such and such.*

Even so, this formulation is much too general to have any particular meaning unless we know what "serious" means. For the "serious" is here the standard, and prior in definition: just as the good is prior in definition to, and the standard by which we judge, the bad. And we have to state the serious so that it fits anyone who takes something seriously, not merely a particular kind of man.

Anyone whosoever, then, will take seriously (1) anything that *seems to him good or evil,* (2) in what seems to him a *considerable degree* (that is, enough to warrant preference and action), (3) in proportion as it seems to him *certain or likely or possible,* and (4) likely to happen *sooner* rather than later; (5) likely to produce or be accompanied by *further* goods or evils, to *increase or decrease* these, or to bring them on *sooner or later;* or (6) anything which indicates that such a thing *has happened, is happening,* or *will happen presently.*

And he will take seriously not merely what regards (7) *himself* and (8) those for whom he has some *concern*, or (9) those on whom his own *pleasure or pain is contingent*, but also (10) those who *resemble* him or (11) whose fortunes *resemble* those likely to befall him. Now, these are all opinions; the opinion that something is serious, therefore, is a *complex* of opinions, containing as its minimum elements opinions as to what is good or bad, in what degree, more certain or less, imminent or not, involving whom. This opinion, like a compound proposition, is false if any one of its constituents is false, and it may also be falsified by something other than a constituent; but in the case of the ridiculous, mere falsification is not enough; that is, it is not enough simply to manifest that something is *not serious*. The falsifying element must not only falsify the opinion, but simultaneously establish *the truth of its contrary*. In other words, when we see something as ridiculous after having taken it seriously, we learn not merely that we were mistaken in taking it seriously, that there was inadequate ground for doing so; we are also impelled to take the contrary view of it, because of a *manifest absurdity*.

It must be observed that by "serious" we mean not merely the "very serious" or the tragic but even any ordinary matter of daily life, anything that we see any value in doing—together with any possibility of doing it—in given circumstances. The ridiculous is then the contrary of this, in some characteristic on which its whole value depends, so that the idea of its value is completely destroyed. The *persons* whom we find ridiculous are those whom we feel we can slight, and slight deservedly and with impunity; to whom, therefore, we feel superiority (although this is not, as Hobbes thought, the cause of our laughter but rather a condition of it) and those who believe differently from us, e.g., take seriously things which we do not. We therefore regard them as *unlike* ourselves. The *frame of mind* in which we are likely to find them ridiculous is very similar to that in which we are easily appeased; one in which we are confident, carefree, and in general disposed to be merry. The *ground* on which something is found ridiculous is always a *particular*, in manifest contrariety to the ground on which we should take that particular action or speech seriously.

But perhaps we should consider this more specifically. Consider the ridiculous *act*, for example: one or more of its circumstances must be contrary to the kind we think is required to make the act serious. That is, the *agent* must be contrary to the kind required to make the act serious, or the *person or thing affected, the manner, instrument used, purpose, result, the time, the place*. Thus an intended act of harm becomes ridiculous upon the evident incapacity of its agent to perform it, as a person of qualities—say, of mind or body—contrary to those of the agent proper for the act; or through its being done to a person upon whom it cannot produce a harmful effect, or upon whom it will produce a beneficial effect instead, or to the wrong person, provided that it does not harm him either—the most common form of this is the kind that "backfires" or "boomerangs" on the agent himself.

We use the term "ridiculous" to cover two quite different cases which I think should be distinguished: that in which the act results from the *character* of the agent—that is, is ridiculous because of some *fault in the agent*—and that in which the act is ridiculous simply because of the agent's *ignorance of circumstances, or because of chance*. In the former both *agent and act* are ridiculous; in the latter, the *act* only. In both the agent may be mistaken; the question is whether he himself is responsible. Sancho is a generally ridiculous character, but in Jean Paul's instance of his clinging to the ditch-side, I should say that the action was not ridiculous but ludicrous; his action was perfectly reasonable given what he knew, and it was not his fault that he did not know the supposed precipice was only a ditch. I make this distinction because it has consequences for our later discussion of comedy. This distinction aside, the ridiculous and the ludicrous resemble each other both in form and in effect: the same contrariety obtains in both, and both may produce laughter. Both involve our anticipation of a standard of seriousness, supposedly applicable in the present instance, together with a manifest opposition to it which destroys that supposition; and it is precisely at the moment when the opposition is manifest that the emotion we are in quest of, the emotion conducive to laughter, is produced.

Indeed, we are now in a position to define that emotion: it is a relaxation, or as Aristotle would say, a *katastasis*, of concern due to a manifest absurdity of the grounds for concern. And we may distinguish three things involved: (1) the apparent or anticipated sequence of circumstances (agent, act, etc.); (2) the factors of apparent seriousness (good or evil of a certain magnitude, etc., as already described); and (3) a real circumstance manifesting the absurdity of attributing (2) to (1). This "real circumstance" is like the factor that betrays something as a lie, instantly replacing belief by disbelief; only here there is involved, not a *truth* merely, but a *feeling* based upon a supposed truth, replaced by its contrary opinion on the discovery.

We can see now why this is a pleasant emotion, for concern of any kind induces tension; the relaxation of concern involves, as Aristotle would say, the settling of the soul into its natural or normal condition, which is always pleasant. Because it *is* pleasant, its anticipation is also pleasant; which is the reason why people are pleased when a favorite comedian is announced, and why one listens to a joke with pleasure, even before the point is reached; and the fulfillment of the anticipation is pleasant as well. Any excess of this emotion, particularly when sudden, will lead, as I have explained, to laughter; because the sudden is always the unexpected and because emotions which are unexpected will always be excessive.

But perhaps all this can be made clearer. Let us consider once more the plight of Sancho in his ditch. Sancho is suffering a real emotion which is based upon the false opinion that the ditch is a cliff. Now all men are alike in their emotions; they differ in what these are based upon. If I contemplate Sancho's fear as such, he is like me, I sympathize with him, I now see the ditch in darkness as very like a precipice, and as a reasonable cause of Sancho's emotion and action. I now take the whole thing seriously, like Sancho. If I contemplate the basis of his emotion, which is an opinion contrary to mine, I see only the difference, I respond only to the absurdity as such, and now see Sancho's fear and action as absurd effects of such a cause as a mere ditch; indeed, I see the relevant differences between ditch and cliff as well. The whole thing now appears ludicrous.

But notice that the difference between the serious and the opposite view is not a matter simply of having or not having a piece of knowledge, as so many theorists have suggested. If I once reflect on the likeness between Sancho and myself, and so share his pain, I shall take his plight seriously whether or not I know the pit in fact is a ditch. On the other hand, if I begin with the difference and reflect on the absurdity of supposing a ditch a pit, I shall not share his pain, and I shall not take his plight seriously even though he is in fact suffering. Indeed, the more earnest he becomes, the more ludicrous he will seem to me; the greater his efforts to save himself, the greater his terror, the funnier he will appear. Here are streams of thought and feeling flowing in opposite directions: the serious, from my sharing his pain to my sharing his view of its cause, even though I know that this is false; the comic, from my rejection of his view to rejection of the pain which is its effect, even though I know that this is real. And this difference of the currents carrying us does not mean merely that we are going in opposite directions; it has made us creatures of different, indeed contrary, worlds, so unlike that I take pleasure in his pain.

The basis of the ridiculous and the ludicrous, therefore, is the *unlike*. (This is why the odd, the eccentric, the quaint, the "original"—as they used to say in the eighteenth century —are so common in comedy; and certainly it is part of the reason for the perpetual exaggerations of comedy.) We naturally consult ourselves as standards; for example, what each man thinks wise is what corresponds to *his* conception of wisdom—and in the present instance, we judge in terms of what is *like* us. It is often said the comic involves taking an objective view of something; but this is false, unless by "objectively viewed" we mean "seen as we should not have seen it were we the victim"—in other words, "viewed as unlike ourselves."

Unlike: but he must also be *like* in some respects, or we should never find him ridiculous. As we approach the wholly unlike, we approach the monstrous, and the monstrous is never ridiculous. Moreover, it is the likeness which supplies the standard with which we must compare him in order to dismiss him or his act or speech entirely—that is, in order to find him ridiculous. To begin with, the *primary* ridiculous is always human; other beings—animals for instance—are only secondarily ridiculous, either by analogy to the human, or by some other relation to the human. There is therefore the matter of *specific* likeness. Again, the ridiculous is *always particular*—and the particular act which is performed must be enough like a given serious act for us to think of it as such, so that we may see its *unlikeness* in the very respect on which its value as action depends. And the basic unlikeness—the *basic* unlikeness—is always an opposition of values, and takes one or both of two forms: an opposition of views on the possibility or probability of the completed act, and an opposition of views on the worth of the act. For example, the ridiculous person thinks something probable when we think it impossible, or vice versa, and he thinks it matters when we think it does not. He is in earnest, and takes something seriously; we relax from our seriousness through seeing that the serious does not apply.

It should be perfectly evident, then, that no theory of this subject can possibly be complete unless it takes the laugher (subject) as well as the laughed-at (object) into account, and that the theories which considered one but not the other are therefore incomplete. Indeed, in nature the ridiculous always occurs by *chance:* the chance presence and witnessing of the act on the part of an observer who chances to have the contrariety of views just mentioned. As an act in itself apart from an observer, it is simply wrong; it is only incidentally ridiculous.

Since the observer is necessarily involved, and involved by a basic contrariety to the ridiculous man, two further things must be taken into account: his relation to the object of laughter as either friend or enemy or stranger, and the kind of standard which he applies. Both of these factors affect the *quality* of the comic. The rallying and teasing that goes on among friends is obviously of a very different order from the mockery and jeering of enemies, and the kind of standard entailed is clearly related to the distinction between high and low wit, or polished and vulgar wit. These matters have important consequences for comedy, and I shall examine these later.

Leaving these aside for the moment, we may say that the ridiculous person, then, is always inferior, in a way which obviates the possibility of taking him seriously—that is, as the object of any serious emotion; he is not merely bad, but bad in a way which renders him worthless or of no account even as bad. Yet Cicero and the others who have identified the ridiculous with baseness (*turpitudo*) are clearly mistaken. It is true that comedy is crowded with misers and cowards and hypocrites and such; but there is nothing comic in miserliness or cowardice or hypocrisy as such; nor is there in intellectual faults such as folly or ignorance. These are comic only in the sense that they are conducive to particular actions which are ridiculous. The miser and the coward allow their governing passions to run away with their reason, the fool and the ignoramus are deficient in rational principle itself, but they are not on this account ridiculous. Indeed, even a miser would be critical of the comic miser, and a coward of the comic coward, though they share the same fault and have the same general ends in view; the actions of the comic types are wrong even from the point of view of their own vices.

The persons I have called *ludicrous* are not, however, necessarily inferior, although their actions and speeches may appear identical with those of the ridiculous; for, as I have said, they are not to blame; their absurdities are due either to a natural mistake or to some deception, insofar as they are agents. Insofar as they are patients—that is, merely involved in something ludicrous, without actually doing anything ludicrous—they are so involved either through chance or through someone's contrivance. People are ludicrous or ridiculous in appearance as well as in speech or action: because of bodily or facial structure, or facial expression, or gesture, or motion, or physical activity, or dress, because these either are signs of actual conditions of the person, or resemble such signs. Thus a lugubrious expression may be ridiculous under certain circumstances because it denotes the absence of a sense of humor; or an expression which is not lugubrious may under the same circumstances be ridiculous because it resembles a lugubrious one. Finally, that which is a sign of the ludicrous, or which resembles it, is also ludicrous; we may call this the principle of analogy.

These three things—the ridiculous, the ludicrous, and that which is taken as one or the other because of analogy—constitute, I believe, the complete list of objects of the kind of laughter-emotion we are discussing—that is, of things we *laugh at*, in the strictest sense of this expression. But as often as not we do not use it strictly; we apply it to something quite opposite as well; we say we laugh at a witty remark, and we often speak of such remarks as ridiculous or ludicrous.

Such remarks, however, require a quite different analysis. Wit is a certain intellectual excellence; no one was ever thought ridiculous in the sense we have been considering because he was a man of wit, or ever ridiculed on the ground that he was witty. The fact is that we laugh *with* the wit, *at* the butt; and we *laugh at* the witty remark only in the sense that it exposes something as ridiculous or ludicrous. As I see it, wit operates in *four modes: practical wit*, in which the wit induces the butt to betray himself as ridiculous by his own action (practical joking is the crudest form of this); *mimicry*—that is, the wit ridicules someone by mimicking him; *witty speech*, which is what we usually think of; and the *witty act* used *instead of speech*, since we may convey a meaning by action as well as by words. When the wit is successful, we laugh, and notice that we are *like* the wit: we take the same view of the victim that the wit in fact does, although commonly enough he will himself pretend a view quite different to his real one.

Wit and butt are, however, not necessarily permanent distinctions. Very frequently a simpleton says something to make the wit the butt of his own jokes, and in repartee the persons engaged play wit and butt alternately. This may seem inconsistent with my earlier remark that the wit is never ridiculed; in fact it is not, for the wit commits a particular ridiculous action when he exposes himself to the retort.

We laugh also at what we call *humorous* remarks and behavior. These differ from wit, as proceeding not from the actualization of acute intellect but from general affability. The devices upon which these depend are such simple ones as exaggeration, irony, understatement, the deprecation of any seriousness, and the like; and the effects produced are related rather to the frame of mind conducive to the laughter-emotion than to the emotion itself, although that emotion may indeed result. As we are affected by it, we are drawn into a relaxed, indulgent view of things; neither is the humorous man ridiculous nor does he make anything actually ridiculous; he takes a humane view wherever possible.

Allied to the humorous, as promoting a similar frame of mind, are the gay, the lighthearted, the playful, the joyous; these involve "infectious" or "contagious" conditions, generally speaking, and may arise not merely from humans but from animals or anything else in which we happen to fancy these characteristics, as Wordsworth did in a field of daffodils. But such things—together with the charming things done or said by children, for example—carry us rather into joy; and when they cause laughter, cause the laughter of joy. And that

—while not opposed to the comic—is really different from it.

Properly speaking, then, the comic includes only the ridiculous, the ludicrous, the things which are taken as such by analogy, the witty, and the humorous. All of these, differ as they may, have a common characteristic: their minimization of the claim of some particular thing to be taken seriously, either by reducing that claim to absurdity, or by reducing it merely to the negligible in such a way as to produce pleasure by that very minimization. The comic object must, first of all, then, be something which may be thought to present such a claim: for what does not exist cannot be minimized. Thus, something that we already regard as of no value whatsoever, either in itself or in relation to anything else, is not a comic object; it is rather an object of indifference. The comic object must either excite some degree of desire or aversion, or afford the basis *for the inception* of some emotion, or promote the anticipation of one of these; it may simply evoke curiosity or wonder, which involve a desire to know, or it may present us with something apparently fearful or pathetic. On the other hand, it must not arouse desire or aversion or emotion to such a degree that they cannot easily be extinguished. For it is precisely by the destruction or annihilation of the *ground* of the desire or aversion or emotion that the comic operates.

Let us illustrate. Suppose something is presented to me as remarkable; it will then excite my curiosity and wonder; I shall take it seriously; if my curiosity about it is satisfied, I shall of course be gratified; and I shall take that seriously too. If my curiosity is not satisfied, I shall continue to wonder, and I will be serious in that too. Here we are dealing with the fulfillment or frustration of desire; and whether the desire is fulfilled or not, its ground remains unchanged, as do my ideas of the desire and its object; I am in earnest about the whole thing. But if I find that the object is neither an object of desire or aversion or any serious emotion—that the thing in question was the *contrary* of the wonderful and inexplicable, or else a manifest hoax—I shall at once lapse into a condition contrary to that of being in earnest; and this is the comic reaction.

This is the psychological formula, if I may use such an expression, of a great many jokes: something apparently extraordinary is recounted, exciting your curiosity and wonder; then you discover either that what you thought extraordinary was the very opposite, or that the whole was a matter of cock and bull.

So much, then, for the general theory of the comic. It is primarily man who is laughed at, and it is only man who laughs; and perhaps it should not much astonish us that we seem to have found that the comic is only a particular sort of relation among human beings. We shall find the same principles at work, I think, when we come to the comic, not as happening by chance in nature, but as arranged by art.

CHAPTER II

The Poetics of Comedy

I

In investigating the nature of the comic, we found that it was not so much a question of laughter as of the restoration of the mind to a certain condition. This, we said, was a pleasant, or rather a euphoric condition of freedom from desires and emotions which move men to action, and one in which we were inclined to take nothing seriously and to be gay about everything. The *transition* to this state was effected through a special kind of relaxation of concern: a *katastasis*, as I called it, of concern through the annihilation of the concern itself—not by the substitution for desire of its contrary, aversion, nor by the replacement, say, of fear, by the contrary emotion of hope, which is also serious, but by the conversion of the *grounds* of concern into absolutely nothing. I gave you as an example a common form of joke which presents something as remarkable, only to disclose that it was something either perfectly ordinary or else impossible; so that it removed our concern—in this case our curiosity—not by gratifying it but by destroying the curiosity itself. This was produced either by the ridiculous or the ludicrous themselves, or by the wit or humor which exposed them to us as such; and I went on to show what things we take seriously, and in what respects the ridiculous and the ludicrous are their contraries. I said a good deal more, and shall have a good deal more to say about these matters; for the moment this will suffice.

Our present problem is the nature of comedy; and many critics have insisted that we must distinguish between the comic and comedy itself. They are quite right: the comic is a certain quality, and comedy, as I am taking it, is a certain form of drama. The former may apply to things outside art; the latter, to art alone.

In my first chapter I quoted L. C. Knights as saying that the discussion of the essence of tragedy or comedy was unprofitable. What he means, I presume, is that the discussion of universals cannot provide us with a knowledge of such characteristics of the individual as are unique with that individual. This is rather obvious but perfectly true, and it has nothing to do with the profit or lack of it in the discussion of essences. And we need not worry about the possibility of definition. Anything that exists is not merely a particular thing but also a thing of a certain determinate kind, even if it is the only one of its kind; we may consequently ask, of anything that exists, what kind of thing it is, what its essence is. *Ti esti;* what is it? If we state its essence, we have a definition. We cannot, however, like L. J. Potts, whom I also mentioned, suppose that because the name *comedy* has been applied to *Tristram Shandy* and *Pride and Prejudice* as well as to *The Frogs,* the definition of comedy would result only in "a vague formula." The fact is the other way around: the "vague formula" which would result would *not* be a definition. How can we have a single definition of things which are heterogeneous? If definition is the statement of the nature of something, how can one definition state the natures of things which are different in nature? The correct procedure is rather to distinguish the different applications of the name, and find the diverse natures of the things to which it has been applied. For the term is obviously ambiguous, and this is the only way in which we can remove the ambiguity. That once done, the difficulty disappears.

What is comedy?

It is, first of all, something artificial. It is also something composite; it involves form and matter, and because it is artificial, a form is realized in a certain matter which would not naturally have assumed such a form. Take painting as a parallel; the matter here is color, but the colors do not by nature assume the figures of a fish on a plate or a bouquet of flowers. If they did so of inherent necessity, paintings would be natural objects, and there would be no art of painting. But necessity is not involved; only possibility. That is, it is possible that the colors should assume the form of flowers and it is possible that they should not, for possibility always means the possibility of opposites; and it is within the areas of possibility that all the various arts operate. When anything is a composite, it does not properly take its name from any of its constituents, but from the composite itself; thus we should not properly call the painting either "colors" or "flowers," for it is something different from either: it is rather a likeness of flowers, and it is neither a natural likeness such as flowers of the same species bear to each other (for these all have the same matter) nor the accidental likenesses sometimes produced by natural forces—such as the Great Stone Face, and the ship-like rocks in the Wisconsin Dells, which are called the Navy Yard. In a word, it is an imitation. And comedy is similarly an imitation.

Of course, in saying this we have at once loosed the dogs of war; we have just committed ourselves to a crucial doctrine in Aristotle's *Poetics,* and any number of people will arise to condemn us for having espoused a doctrine which, according to them, is certainly obsolete and was probably never true in the first place. I can only reply that a truth is never obsolete, and so we need be concerned only with the question of its truth. Now, the objections turn on the observation that art does not always imitate nature. It is a mistaken objection; the question is not whether all art imitates nature (for Aristotle never said that) but whether *some* art imitates. Disproof of the doctrine therefore must establish that no object of art bears a likeness in form to some form of nature. So far no one has thought to establish that.

In his book *Aristotle's Poetics: The Argument* (in which, by the way, the *Poetics* turns out not to be worth much as argument), Professor Gerald F. Else finds the term imitation a hopelessly ambiguous one; indeed Aristotle is "notoriously inconsistent" in the use of his cardinal terms. Here again the objection is badly taken. *Imitation* is a relative term, for an imitation is always an *imitation of something,* just as a parent is always a parent *of* an offspring, and a teacher a teacher *of* a pupil; but there is no ambiguity simply because a relative term may be applied to different correlatives. The term may also be used substantially, as when we say comedy and tragedy are imitations. When the term is used substantially, it applies (for Aristotle) only to artificial things; no natural *substance* is essentially an imitation of anything else, however much it resembles it. A son, for example, is not the imitation of his father, however like him he may be; and in cases of natural mimicry (say, of protective coloration) where the mantis looks like a leaf, the mantis is not the imitation of a leaf; it is an insect. Imitation may be of the particular or universal. Imitation of the particular is of course "copying"; but tragedy and comedy are not "copies"; nor is there the least inconsistency in calling them imitations nevertheless.

And imitation admits of degree as well; so that there is no inconsistency in saying that tragedy and epic are both imitations and that tragedy is more imitative than epic. All of these charges of ambiguity and inconsistency stem from confusions as to what ambiguity and inconsistency are. Inconsistency entails ultimate contradiction, but there can be no contradiction unless affirmation and denial involve the same senses of the words employed; and terms are not ambiguous unless there is uncertainty in their application.

But to return to positive argument: if imitation involves (1) a likeness of form (not essential but sensible form) (2) in some matter other than that in which the form is naturally found, this must be done (3) *somehow,* and (4) for the sake of something. The *what is imitated* (the object of imitation), the *in what matter imitated* (the means of imitation), the *how imitated* (the manner of imitation), and the *for sake of what* (this last is the *dynamis* of which Aristotle speaks at the very beginning of the *Poetics*)—these are the four causes of imitation in general: formal, material, efficient, and final; and it is through differentiating these that any species of imitation (comedy, for example) is to be defined. In the definition of natural species, only genus and differentia are required; in the case of anything which does not exist by nature, no natural genus or differentia exists, and consequently these can have their essence stated only in terms of the differentiated causes which make them what they are. Thus Aristotle, distinguishing a group of arts which all involved the same general means, distinguished these as they employed these means differently, and as they imitated different objects, and in a different manner.

We must realize that the differentiation of the arts according to means, object, manner, and power *(dynamis)* is one of permanent validity. It is true the distinctions as given by

Aristotle may be too general; for example, the distinction of manner of imitation into narrative, dramatic, and mixed is too general when applied to modern novels; it will not distinguish the narrative methods of Henry James, Melville, Joyce, Forster, and Faulkner, for instance, from that of Homer. But this fact does not invalidate the basic distinction; on the contrary, we must build on it by differentiating the various narrative methods which have developed. I am aware of how much the *Poetics* has been under attack on all these points. But attack here must demonstrate one of three things: (1) that there are no works of art exhibiting likeness of form to any natural object; (2) that if there are works which do, they do so accidentally and not essentially; (3) that the specific causal analysis here entailed has no bearing on the essence of art. If any one of these three things is proved, the *Poetics* must be absolutely discredited; if not, the *Poetics* must be taken as valid and permanently valid, however art may develop in future, and all objections are either trivial or irrelevant. Do not misunderstand me: I am not saying that the *Poetics* offers the *only* valid approach to art; I am saying that it involves *a* valid approach to the kinds of art with which it is concerned.

Although imitations are artificial likenesses, the pleasure taken in imitations has its root in human nature. Man, Aristotle tells us, is the most imitative of animals; he enjoys imitating and witnessing imitations because he learns thus, and learning is natural, and whatever is natural is pleasant. Man learns through *likeness;* it is through likeness that memories of similars become experience (*Met.* I.1) and by likeness that the universals with which science and art are conversant arise out of experience *(empeiria).* The pleasure involved in the recognition of likeness explains our pleasure in simile and metaphor also, for these involve perception of a likeness hitherto unobserved, and the analogical metaphor is the most effective since it goes beyond specific or general likeness (*Rhet.* III.10). (Incidentally, this also explains our indifference to or displeasure with *trite* metaphors and similes.) Imitation always sets particulars before us (for example, an imitation of action must set particular actions before us, a certain individual doing such and such); but in developed art, it exhibits particulars which reveal the universal through the particular; it is in this sense that Aristotle speaks of poetry as more philosophic than history. A cognitive pleasure, and cognition of a universal truth, is clearly present here as basic; and here Aristotle differs sharply from Plato, for whom imitations imply deception and falsification in such degree as they are removed from the idea. We must observe, however, that this by no means accounts, in his view, for all the pleasures we receive from art, or for the pleasure peculiar to any given art. The matter of the poetic arts is also pleasant to man, because natural to him; he has an instinct for speech, harmony, and rhythm.

Pleasure in imitation is distinct from pleasure in the natural object imitated; thus what is repulsive in nature may be pleasing in imitation, and on the contrary, an imitation which pleases merely because it brings to mind a pleasing object does not please as imitation, but as a stimulant to pleasant recollection. On the other hand, one absolutely unacquainted with the object imitated also cannot be pleased with the imitation as an imitation; he can only be pleased with the materials, e.g., colors and figures as such, since he has failed to perceive the form of imitation through ignorance of what it was *like*. This is true whether the imitation is of particulars (as in mere mimicry) or of universals, as in art proper.

In art, thus, we react not to the object imitated, but to the object *as imitated;* to the likeness, not to the original. That likeness may present the object as better or worse, while still remaining *like;* for example, generally the portraitist represents his subject as better, and the caricaturist as worse, though both make likenesses. Upon this possibility, in fact, the possibility of tragedy and of comedy is dependent.

In imitation a form is actualized out of a matter naturally alien to it (the means or artistic medium; a matter that has no natural tendency to assume that form); consequently the work is to be accounted for neither in terms of the natural causes relative to its object, nor in terms of those relative to the means employed. In nature a tree grows on a hill and a bird builds a nest in it, and we should explain this in terms of natural causes, but quite different causes would be relevant to a picture of this; for instance, we should not say of the picture that the hill supported the tree and the tree the nest, for the painted hill and tree in fact support nothing. The unity, even, of these is different; a picture is not unified because it represents a single object only, and an object is not a natural unit because it appears in a single picture. The wholeness and completeness of object and imitation differ in the same way; the picture may be whole and complete although what it represents is not whole and complete in nature. Similarly with the medium; the picture is not one or whole or complete because it actualizes one potentiality of the medium, or actualizes it wholly.

Yet the imitation is related to its object in the sense that it is like some sensible form of it, and to its means in that it is possible as an actualization because the means has certain potentialities. A given artistic means can represent an object only in two ways: through direct simulation or through simulation by signs. Any colored plane figure can be imitated through direct simulation in a painting, because the color and the figure are possible to the means as such; this is likeness; but objects as masses in space can be imitated only signally on a piece of canvas; the third dimension is depicted by signs. The idea of distance is conveyed, not by portraying distance itself, but by depicting the effects which distance would have, and which are consequently the signs of distance. Thus the painter depicts distance by the occlusion of one thing by another, by proportional diminution in size (perspective), by gradual loss of detail as objects are supposedly distant, by the diminution in intensity of color, etc. When a given means can depict neither directly nor by sign, it cannot imitate; it is impossible to depict a face by musical tones because these do not have position in space and cannot signify position in space, and a succession of sounds cannot be depicted by a painter because figure and color have neither the attributes of sound, such as pitch and intensity, nor attributes which can signify these. Thus Aristotle tells us in the *Politics* that music may imitate movements and states in the soul because rhythm involves movement and stasis; this is direct likeness. Painting and sculpture, on the other hand, can depict emotion and moral character only through signs; for example, anger or moral nobility can be depicted only by showing the distinctive effects which these have on facial expression or bodily posture.

The natural properties of any medium permit it to imitate relatively few things directly, and a great many more signally. Imitation by signs may employ natural or artificial signs. These latter depend not upon the natural properties of the medium but upon convention. For example, in Noh drama, the hand passed before the mask indicates weeping; this is an artificial sign of grief; it is possible only through convention, and can be understood only by those who know the convention.

Now, imitation gives pleasure; and there are two ways in which we can be given pleasure; either by the presentation of what is naturally pleasant to us, or by the removal of something painful. Thus we are pleased not merely by what accords with our nature and desires and habits but by being freed from anything counter to these; for example, it is pleasant to be freed from compulsion of any kind, such as slavery or imprisonment, though slavery and imprisonment are not pleasant. Imitation may be of objects either naturally pleasant or naturally unpleasant, and still give pleasure; only in the case of the naturally unpleasant, there occurs a particular phenomenon which we must give some attention.

For we confront here the famous and much fought-over doctrine of *catharsis.* Let me say, to begin with, that this doctrine seems to me far less difficult of interpretation, and one which affords far less room for speculation, than is generally supposed. The term occurs only once* in the *Poetics,* in the definition of tragedy; and many—Professor Else, for example—find it unprepared for and followed by no particular consequence. The term also occurs in the last book of the *Politics;* and Robertello was the first, I believe, to patch out a meaning for the term on that basis. There have been many interpretations—the medical interpretations alone range from allopathy to homeopathy—and it would be a long and perhaps unnecessary task to review them all here. Let us consider the matter directly. In the first place, it is not true that the term is unprepared for: the term catharsis is simply a specification, to tragedy, of the term *dynamis* in the opening sentence of the *Poetics.* It is specified in two ways in chapter 4: first, by the observation that even the unpleasant may please in imitation, and second by the consideration of the

---

* Actually twice; but the second use is in the sense of the religious purification of Orestes (*Poetics,* 1555b 19).

development of tragedy. Again, Aristotle tells us that his definition has been "collected" from the foregoing matter (*apolabontes autes ek ton eiremenon ton gignomenon horon tes ousias,* "collecting the definition of its nature which results from the aforesaid"). It would be curious indeed if Aristotle should have been so careless in so important a matter as a definition—and particularly in the part which states the final cause, which is the most important for him of all causes. Nor is catharsis without further consequence: it is manifestly connected with the question of what the poet should aim at in the construction of his plots, for this is the final cause, in chapters 13 and 14. Here he is concerned with the removal of the morally repellent *(to miaron) by the proper construction of plot.* The *term* is dropped; the concept continues. But indeed this is standard Aristotelian procedure; for example, the term *hexis* is similarly transmuted into *arete* in the *Nicomachean Ethics.* However, the point is clear: the imitation of a fearful and pitiful action may give pleasure *if* the imitation is properly made *(ei mellei kalos hexein he poiesis).* Catharsis is thus effected by proper construction.

We may take a grave or a lighthearted view of human life and actions; tragedy develops out of the grave view as comedy does out of the lighthearted. If we take the grave view, life is full of perils and misfortunes which evoke in us fear and pity; if we take the lighthearted view, there is nothing to be greatly concerned about. It is not the events by themselves which are matter for gravity or levity; it is the view taken of them. *Convention* may determine that this is a solemn matter, and not to be joked about; but so far as things themselves are concerned, death, murder, rape, incest are no less matter for comedy than for tragedy. The Oedipus legend served Sophocles as a tragic subject; it would be quite as possible to make it into comedy. When we say, thus, that tragedy imitates a serious action, we mean that it imitates an action *which it makes serious;* and comparably, comedy imitates an action *which it makes a matter for levity*.

If it is now clear what imitation is and what catharsis is, it should be clear what comedy is and what it effects. It has no catharsis, since all the kinds of the comic—the ridiculous and ludicrous, for example—are naturally pleasant. Tragedy exhausts pity and fear by arousing these emotions to their utmost and by providing them with their most perfect objects; it excites concern and directs it into its proper channel; it brings the mind into its normal condition by energizing its capacity for painful emotion. Comedy, on the other hand, removes concern by showing that it was absurd to think that there was ground for it. Tragedy endows with worth; comedy takes the worth away. Tragedy exhibits life as directed to important ends; comedy as either not directed to such ends, or unlikely to achieve them.

If we call action of the latter sort *valueless,* we may define comedy as an imitation of valueless action, in language, performed and not narrated, effecting a katastasis of concern through the absurd. To this definition we must add such qualifications of magnitude, completeness, etc., as Aristotle does; but the main points are, I hope, clear.

On this account of the whole, it is clear that comedy must consist of the same number of parts as tragedy—that is, the six parts of plot, character, thought, diction, music, and spectacle—but that these parts cannot be of the same quality as those of tragedy, for in that case tragedy and comedy would be identical.

We must discuss this point later; for the moment, let us consider the comic action and the kind of personage we properly call comic. I have just called the comic action "worthless" or "valueless." This is a translation of the Greek *phaulos*. I may explain this, perhaps, by contrasting it with the tragic action. The tragic action produces pity and fear— "pity," says Aristotle, "for the man suffering undeserved misfortune; fear for the man like ourselves." The comic action is the precise opposite of this: the comic character, as I argued earlier, is *unlike us, insofar as he is comic,* and the misfortunes, insofar as they are comic, either are not grave or are deserved. The comic action, thus, neutralizes the emotions of pity and fear to produce the *contrary*—again I must insist, not the negative or contradictory but *the contrary*— of the serious.

We must also observe that not every serious action is tragic, and that, comparably, not every "worthless" action is comic; a tragic action is a serious action which has been constructed so as to have the power or *dynamis* of producing pity and fear, and the comic action is the worthless action which has been so constructed as to have the power of the emotion conducive to laughter. Moreover, not even every serious action which arouses pity and fear is tragic; but only that kind which catharts these emotions; and similarly, not every worthless action, even when involving laughter, is comic, but only the kind which effects *katastasis* or relaxation, i.e., by affording the perfect object for this emotion.

The question may arise of what we may mean by "the proper object of emotion"; for obviously people pity or fear different things, and some take seriously what others do not. The multiplicity and diversity of reaction has often been cited as an impassable obstacle to any general theory. Perhaps it is not impassable after all. Surely here as elsewhere we must take the sound as a standard by which we judge the unsound, and not mingle all together as if they had an equal claim to consideration; it would be foolish, for instance, to accept the word of a man with poor vision as equally authoritative with that of the man whose vision is excellent. Here, similarly, we must take the word of the brave man rather than that of a coward as to what is really fearful, and thus generally the word of the virtuous person; so that what is really pitiful or fearful, or serious or comic, is what is so in the judgment of the man of practical wisdom. Hence, while anything may be ridiculed, it is only the really ridiculous which is *properly* ridiculed; and it is only proper ridicule that really produces the comic response, for it alone produces pleasure through the ridiculous as such. Otherwise ridicule either stems from what is unpleasant or produces displeasure; for example, a great many jokes are really kinds of aggression; those who laugh at them laugh because they feel hatred for the object ridiculed, and hatred is always of something painful; and other people are offended by jokes of this order. Those who take pleasure in jokes or ridicule of this kind are pleased because it is pleasant to think that the object of their hatred is utterly valueless, though the fact that they hate it shows that they are pained by it and therefore do attribute to it a value which they are unwilling to admit.

From these observations it is evident that as imitations tragedy and comedy offer us likenesses of the tragic and ridiculous which we recognize as such, and in their universal aspect, although manifested through particulars; and that it is upon such recognition that our emotional responses are contingent. Thus imitation affords the pleasure both of learning—through recognizing the ridiculous thing precisely as ridiculous, for example—and of emotional satisfaction; though the latter is clearly contingent upon the former. In their proper nature, therefore, the arts offer us proper moral perceptions. They cannot in so doing make us virtuous, for virtue is a habit which can only be produced by action; they can supply us with knowledge of what is good or bad, whether we act on it or not; and they do this not for the sake of such knowledge but in fulfillment of their own nature. From this their ethical and political value is easily apparent, as well as why they are helpful to good societies and governments and dangerous to the bad.

To put this a little differently: comedy and tragedy differ basically in the value which they induce us to set upon the actions which they depict; and one and the same act, seen in contrary lights, produces contrary effects. This is surely what Shaw had in mind in the Preface to *Saint Joan,* when, speaking of her burning, he remarks: "At such murders the angels weep; but the gods laugh at the murderers." The angels see the action in terms of the undeserved anguish and death of the victim; the gods see it in terms of the folly which motivates it and which makes it absurdly incapable of achieving its proposed end. In their less than divine wisdom the angels respond with more than human pity; the wiser gods see only the folly of man.

Tragedy and comedy are contraries, thus, in that the former sets something before us as supremely serious, and evokes our extremest concern, while the latter disavows all cause for concern; and comedy often produces its characteristic relaxation by treating lightly things which we take most seriously. I have said there are jokes of aggression or attack; there are also jokes of defense. In writing this book, for example, I looked over a number of anthologies of Jewish jokes and found to my astonishment that a great many dealing with Russian or Nazi persecutions of the Jews were fairly contemporary with such persecutions. I was puzzled by this until I saw that this was perfectly consistent with my hypothesis; they had to laugh or else to weep, and they had enough weeping; they could master their nightmare only by laughing at it. Similarly, jokes about war and soldiery seem to spring up in times of war; and the same principle seems to account for the fact that religious or ethnic or national jokes, as well as jokes about social taboos, greatly outnumber the jokes of pure fun; they seem to indicate our need to take lightly things that otherwise we take seriously.

Perhaps these are rather matters for the psychologist and the social scientist; they are relevant here, however, as further indications that—while it would be a rare comedy that evoked no laughter—the comic function is less one of producing laughter than one of producing a lightheartedness and gaiety with which laughter is associated. This is something both deeper and more valuable than laughter; and it involves achieving a state of mind in which we can view human frailties with smiling indulgence. Indeed, it may involve a state like that of a saint or a god; *Saint Joan,* it seems to me, is a comedy for a saint (at least the Saint herself sees it as comedy), while *The Tempest* conveys almost a divine view of human action.

I have opposed comedy to the serious, and thus, it may be thought, have left no room for it in comedy. I do not think that this is the case; except for sheer slapstick and froth and buffoonery, there is always a serious element in comedy. The comic action does not consist wholly in comic incidents; it is comic not in virtué of each and every part being comic but in virtue of its being comic *as a whole;* just as not every character in comedy is comic, necessarily; some are comic in themselves, others only in that they assist in the comedy. Every comedy which is not, in Meredith's phrase, mere hypergelasticism, mere irresponsibility which laughs at anything and everything whether there is a cause of laughter or not (and comedy is no more possible in such circumstances than tragedy is when it takes everything and anything seriously)—every comedy proper, in short, requires us to take certain things seriously so that we may see something else as not to be taken so. The distinction between the important and the unimportant must involve reference to one and the same standard, without which they cannot be distinguished; hence to recognize one is to recognize the other. The particular ways in which comedies involve the serious will become apparent, I trust, in our subsequent analyses of particular plays.

Thus far we have been talking of the *comic quality* of the action; but the action of comedy is also a *dramatic* action, and we must consider what we mean by calling it that. I have discussed this question extensively in *Tragedy and the Theory of Drama;* but rather than repeat or summarize what I said there, I should like to examine it here from a different point of view. A dramatic action is one that is capable of being acted out, that is, represented directly or indirectly by the external behavior of the actors. Direct representation involves the real or the simulated action; for example, the actor may represent eating either by really eating or by going through the motions of eating; thus any physical action may be represented if the actor can do or pretend to do an action *like* it. But that is all that physical action can directly represent: physical action *like it;* so that if acting consisted in nothing further, we could have only plays of physical action. Fortunately, it is possible also to represent indirectly by signs, so that although the actor can never make evident his passions and desires and thoughts as such, he can still represent them by such natural signs as the facial expressions, the postures, gestures, tones of voice, etc., which are the characteristic effects of these internal conditions. He cannot let us see into his heart or his brain, and if he could, we should not know what to make of what we saw there—what X-ray can show us grief in someone's heart? and have us recognize it as what it is? In addition to such natural signs there are also artificial ones which are fixed by convention. Some forms of Oriental drama—Noh, for instance—rely on these, indeed, to an incredible degree, but even Western drama has used them. Eighteenth-century audiences knew what it meant when the heroine came in with her hair down, as nineteenth-century audiences knew what it meant when a girl was blonde or dark.

These are the resources of the actor; and if we can discover similarly the resources of the dramatist, we may shed some light on the nature of dramatic action. I should like to put the matter in terms of an analogy with language, and talk of the grammar and syntax of the drama. The analogy is not so far-fetched as it may seem at first sight. Consider what drama can do. It has subjects (e.g., "Othello" and "Iago") and predicates ("is growing jealous," "is persuading") and it can combine these affirmatively or negatively. If we grant that there are such things as problem-plays and propaganda-plays, it can question or command, so that the interrogative and the imperative are possible to it. Even certain subjunctives are possible to it, e.g., the subjunctive contrary to fact: for example, "Had he not been hindered, Othello would have killed Iago." Limitation and generalization are also possible to it; that is, drama can attach a certain predicate to *some* or *all* of its characters. It can qualify predicates and indicate tense, as "Othello killed Desdemona in ignorance" and "Iago will be tortured." And it can do much more which deserves investigation; but this will suffice, perhaps, to illustrate that, say, the dramatization of a narrative involves translation of the language of the narrative into the "language" of drama; a matter of how this can be "said"—as indeed we say—on the stage.

Experience generally provides us with syntheses; but language itself—I mean real language, not language of the drama—is generally analytic. Experience gives us a man running; language distinguishes between the man and his running, giving each a separate name, and then artificially recouples them to say "The man is running" in order to express the experiential synthesis. Because it fragments experience thus, language must give successive expression even to attributes which are simultaneous in fact. As it proceeds in its course of distinction, it develops two kinds of expressions: those resulting from the distinctions—"significants" or categorematic expressions—and those which indicate how the former are to be connected and correlated—syncategorematics. Thus language itself; but the language of drama reverses this process. It does not give us "Othello is speaking" but Othello-speaking—an experiential synthesis itself, although an artificial one. Attributes that real language can express only successively, action can often render simultaneously; for action is a synthesis. To put this generally, to ask *why* we have the various forms which language develops is to answer the question of how action "speaks," for the principles by which experience is converted into language are identical with those by which language is converted into action. For example, in experience one thing happens later than another; to express this in language we use such an expression as "after"; while action expresses a thing which is "after" another by *having* it happen afterward, in the way of experience itself.

So much for the syntax of drama; as to its "vocabulary," we at once see that it is the inverse of that of the actor. The sphere of the actor is physical action; that of the dramatist, verbal action; thus these arts beautifully complement each other. I have said that whenever the properties of the medium are identical with the properties of the thing to be represented, direct representation is possible; otherwise only indirect representation is possible. The actor works with physical action and can represent directly any bodily movement or act; the dramatist can represent through speech any deed which speech may do—commanding, persuading, threatening, pleading, and the like—and of course declare thought through speech. The actor can represent verbal actions only by signs; the dramatist can represent physical action only by signs. Thus each can either represent what the other cannot, or represent it differently. Each in a sense extends the possibilities of the other.

In discussing the key terms of imitation and catharsis, as well as what is involved in dramatic manner, we have now completed the foundations for the poetics of comedy. We must now see what we can build upon these foundations.

CHAPTER III

The Poetics of Comedy
II

In the preceding chapter, after a good deal of argument, we achieved a definition of comedy. It was modeled—some might say, to the degree of servility—upon Aristotle's famous definition of tragedy. In this respect, it may remind you of the definition in the *Coislinian Tractate*. The *Tractate* is an anonymous piece, written somewhere before the first century B.C. by someone who knew of Aristotle's definition, but —in my opinion, at least—did not quite understand it or its function, for in aping it he assigns to comedy the power of catharsizing, through pleasure and laughter, pleasure and laughter themselves. Why anyone should want to get rid of pleasure or be pleased by getting rid of pleasure, or how he could get rid of pleasure and still have it, he fails to say.

But we also modeled upon Aristotle. And perhaps this explains why there has been so much fussing about a definition. For Aristotle a definition involves not merely—as in our usual sense—the meaning of a word but the essence of a thing, the statement of what it is. If you are going to talk about tragedy as tragedy, or virtue as virtue, or the state as a state, everything depends upon *what* tragedy or virtue or the state *is*. And the whole system of Aristotelian sciences depends upon the possibility of talking, in each science, not about the subject in all its aspects, but in those aspects which related to it *as what it is*.

One way to reach knowledge of what a thing is is to look at it in the process of generation, from origin to completion, considering the conditions which underlie origin and growth and completion; for the completed thing, thus arising, is then seen clearly in its own nature. Once you have been able to state the nature of the complete whole in a definition, you can work from it to find the number and nature and ordering of its specific parts, and treat each of these to see the possibilities of each, and thus the best possibilities.

This, indeed, is the method Aristotle follows in the *Poetics*. The first three chapters treat of causes of imitation in their various differences; chapters four and five trace tragedy from its origin in human instinct (efficient cause) to the completion of the process in a complete product (final cause); from this the nature of the composite whole which is tragedy is "gathered"; and the reasoning now moves from the complete whole to the specific parts, and the causal treatment of each of these. Commentators have often found the *Poetics* a hopeless jumble, at times utterly illogical, because they failed to see the method Aristotle was following; but if you look at the *Poetics* in these terms, you will see the operation of his method quite clearly. We have not followed the very same path he used, partly for convenience of exposition, partly because it was necessary for us, as it was not for Aristotle, to cut through a jungle of confusions and misunderstandings which had grown over and around his noble old road; but we are on much the same course, and have the same destination in mind.

Let me state in full the definition of comedy which I merely sketched earlier. Comedy is the imitation of a worthless action, complete and of a certain magnitude, in language with pleasing accessories differing from part to part, enacted, not narrated, effecting a *katastasis* of concern through the absurd. Since this sounds very odd, I will explain it. By "worthless" or "valueless" action—the Greek word is *phaulos* —I mean one which is of no account, which comes to nothing, so that, on hindsight at least, it would seem foolish to be concerned about it. This is different from ending happily; the *Oresteia* of Aeschylus ends happily, but on hindsight you would never say that you were foolish to have taken the terrors of the House of Atreus seriously. Even the ordinary melodrama or adventure story involves things you are quite right to be concerned about, even though the hero escapes them all. But not comedy; you could call all comedy "Much Ado About Nothing."

"In language with pleasing accessories" is meant to take care of the ornaments of verse and music that tend to accompany comedy in its fullest development; the whole phrase means what it means in Aristotle. The only other difficulty is in the last clause; it stems from my explanations that as the comic was naturally pleasing, there was nothing to cathart, and so no catharsis; rather there was a relaxation or *katastasis* of concern which I have already explained in detail.

From this definition of the whole we derive the same six parts which Aristotle derives from the definition of tragedy, and exactly on the same grounds: namely, plot, character, thought, diction, music, and spectacle. The parts will of course be of a different *quality*, since this is comedy, not tragedy; but I mean by them what Aristotle means by them.

The first three of these, at least, have been the objects of endless confusion and uncertainty; and since upon their interpretation depends all of Aristotle's later treatment of them, that treatment has been the center of controversy, too.

I am not going to enter into full argument on all the various questions; my business here is not to interpret Aristotle but to construct an Aristotelian theory of comedy. I have argued the case at length in *Tragedy and the Theory of Drama*, and in various other places; so that now, with your permission, I shall simply cut the Gordian knot, and say what I think these parts are and what they are not.

Plot is *not* for Aristotle the argument, synopsis, or summary of the play. It is *not* deeds or incidents in abstraction from the agents and patients. It is *not* the myth or legend or history upon which the play is based. It is *not* a chronological list of the enacted events as they occur on the stage. These are all meanings that the term has had—in antiquity, in the Renaissance, even in the present day. But not for Aristotle. The Aristotelian sense of the term is that of a system of acts of a certain moral quality—acts such that a certain moral agency is implicit in them, and hence such that they have a certain moral value as *spoudaios* or *phaulos*, worthy or trivial. The Moor kills Disdemona in Cinthio—or rather assists the killer—and the Moor kills Desdemona in Shakespeare. Are they the same act? They would hardly be so, even if the killings were made, as external actions, more similar than they are. They would hardly be so, that is, unless you are willing to ignore the differences between the moral characters and motives of the two Moors, willing to ignore the difference in moral quality of the two acts. But if you see them as essentially different acts, however externally similar, you also see why Cinthio wrote a mere crime story while Shakespeare wrote a tragedy, and how even their external identity would still entail essential dissimilarity. Incidentally, you also see the Aristotelian meaning of *plot*.

Now, unless you mean plot in this sense, it will not follow

that, as Aristotle holds, it is the most important part of the play; and so, for those who did not take it thus, there are formidable arguments (which, by the way, the dissenters always ignore) to show that plot is prior. Until these are refuted, I shall assume that plot is prior, and continue.

Character means not a person in the drama but moral purpose or choice, as revealed through action or speech; it is that, therefore, in virtue of which we ascribe a certain moral quality to the agents. Thought, finally, is what is revealed by speeches of proof or disproof, or speeches maximizing or minimizing things, or arousing passion; it is not the "thought underlying the play," as we say nowadays. And that much clear, we may in general assume the Aristotelian premises, and go on from there. For clearly the plot, character, and thought—as well as diction and its ornaments—of comedy must be of a different quality from that of the corresponding parts of tragedy; otherwise comedy and tragedy would be the same. And it is these differences that I am eager to investigate.

Mechanically, as we say, it would seem that there is no necessary difference between the tragic or comic or any other plot generally compared. They should all be wholes, and unified, and complete; they all involve universal actions set before us in terms of particular actions—that is to say, involve necessity and probability rather than mere chance, although we shall have to look at this matter again; they should all involve the proper magnitude and proportion of parts if they are to be beautiful, or well constructed.

Yet such general correspondence must not mislead us into supposing that we can discuss comedy by simple adaptations of what Aristotle says about tragedy. That is what got the author of the *Coislinian Tractate* into difficulty. For example, all plots may be simple or complex; Aristotle prefers the complex plot for tragedy; does it follow that the comic plot is better if complex, or, by the opposition of contraries, better if simple? Mr. Paul Lauter, in the able introduction to his anthology, *Theories of Comedy*, suggests the latter.

We shall be in a better condition to judge if we take in mind the difference between simple and complex plots, and the grounds of Aristotle's preference. The simple is in general for Aristotle that which is not divisible into parts, except arbitrarily; the complex is that which is divisible into parts. Continuous movement in one direction is simple; a movement which changes direction is complex, for it divides, at the point of change, into two parts. A simple plot moves steadily in one direction, i.e., of prosperity or adversity, and cannot, of itself, effect surprise; only the complex plot, moving first in one direction and then in the opposite one, can do this. Pity and fear are most effectively felt when they are produced by a probable but unexpected event, for wonder is then evoked; hence Aristotle prefers the complex plot.

Whether it is also better for comedy is to be settled not by opposing contraries but by considering the function of comedy. If this is the *katastasis* of concern through the absurd, as we said, clearly this is also most effective when unexpected, and hence people laugh hardest when they suddenly are struck with a sense of the absurd, and hence those who know how to tell a joke know they must mislead their listeners; no one is pleased by the joke the end of which he anticipates or knows. Indeed, theorists, since Madius at least, have tended to insist on the element of surprise. The complex plot is thus better for comedy, too. The greater effect is produced not by wonder but by the collapse of it. The preposterous is to comedy what wonder is to tragedy.

Indeed, it seems that surprise is more necessary for comedy than it is for tragedy. Comedy tends, too, to have many more reversals. Of course it entails discovery scenes as well; but does it have scenes of suffering—pathos—of its own, to parallel the tragic pathos? On first sight it would appear that it does not, for pathos is requisite in tragedy because the actual sight of suffering increases pity, and comedy is not evocative of pity. But on reflection, we find that scenes of comic suffering —fear where there is no cause for fear, anxiety where there is no cause for anxiety, embarrassment, desperation, absurd beatings, etc., are in fact among the funniest in comedy; and so we must have comic suffering.

But this and other points may be clearer if we consider how the comic plot ought to be contrived to fulfill its function. When, in chapter 13 of the *Poetics*, Aristotle treats of the parallel problem for tragedy, he considers the possible combinations of different agents with different changes of fortune and eliminates those which cannot discharge the tragic function. He is left, thus, with a single formula for the tragic plot involving a single kind of change of fortune, and a single kind of agent: a change from happiness to misery on the part of a man neither preëminently good nor very wicked, "the intermediate sort of personage . . . not preëminently virtuous and just, whose misfortune, however, comes not from vice or depravity but by some error of judgment." The tragic hero is better rather than worse, and must have something to lose.

Aristotle's remark in chapter 5 that the ridiculous is the harmlessly or painlessly bad or ugly has invariably been treated as a definition. It is not a definition; Aristotle would never have permitted a definition with a negative differentia, for a negative term is always ambiguous and hence can state the nature of nothing. What it is, instead, is a placing of the ridiculous person between extremes, precisely comparable to the device which permits the identification of the tragic hero. But we should be hasty indeed if on this basis we proceeded to construct a single formula for the comic plot. There is no such singleness of the ridiculous character as there is of the tragic. The ridiculous character may be morally sound but intellectually deficient, through folly, madness, stupidity, or ignorance (this includes, of course, plain inexperience); he may be clever but morally deficient or he may be deficient both intellectually and morally. What is more, the agent in any one of these three classes may operate in the action from good motives or bad. Again, as we saw in our first chapter, the ridiculous does not exhaust the whole of the comic; there is also the ludicrous man, to say nothing of the wit; and each of these may act from good motives or bad. If we are to be content with the issue of his actions—and if there is to be the comic *katastasis* of concern we must be content—each of these agents must receive his deserts. (There are exceptions to this which I will consider in Chapter V.)

The ten possibilities that seem thus to result really reduce, however, to four: plots of folly or plots of cleverness, with the agent rewarded or punished according to his deserts.* I am calling "plots of folly" all those in which the agent acts in error, for whatever reason, and "plots of cleverness" all those in which the stratagems of the agent produce the comic action. This seems to me a real distinction, since we respond differently to cleverness and folly; and on the same ground, the deserts of the agent, as well- or ill-intentioned, are relevant as affecting our responses. (You may recognize, in this cleverness-folly distinction, our old friends the wit and the

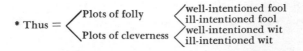

* Thus = Plots of folly — well-intentioned fool / ill-intentioned fool
Plots of cleverness — well-intentioned wit / ill-intentioned wit

butt—for the ridiculous and ludicrous types fuse into the butt.) To give examples: the *Thesmophoriazusae* of Aristophanes has a folly-plot in which the fool is well-intentioned, for Mnesilochus, in trying to help Euripides, gets into trouble by being persuaded to disguise himself as a woman and attend a female festival. Sganarelle in Molière's *The Forced Marriage* (*Le mariage forcé*) is an ill-intentioned fool, for he wishes to break off his marriage merely out of fear. Molière's *The Flying Doctor (Le Médecin volant)* is a plot of cleverness with a well-intentioned wit, for the action flows from Sganarelle's stratagems to save the lovers; Aristophanes' *Peace* and *Lysistrata* are of the same order. Finally, Jonson's *Volpone* and *The Alchemist* have plots of cleverness in which the wits have bad intentions; they are swindlers.

Now, if we can find the most elementary forms of comic plot, we shall be in a position to discuss all others; for the most elaborate plots in the world are simply built out of these elements. I shall assume for the moment that we are talking of consecutive plots, although there are other types —that is, those in which incident follows incident as effect from cause; and in that case, the most elementary form is that in which there is a single agent, all other characters being passive, who performs a single act which causes its single consequence. On what conditions, then, does this elementary plot effect its comic function for each of the four types we have distinguished?

We may state it as follows: for the ill-intentioned fool there must be failure; for the well-intentioned fool, success; for the ill-intentioned clever man, failure, and success for the well-intentioned one. Now, in life the fool fails probably and the clever man succeeds probably, and when they do not it is as a result of accident or chance; but in comedy mere chance should be replaced by a kind of reverse probability: that is, a probability systematically opposite to natural probability. You have this sort in *Through the Looking-Glass*. Having things happen by *mere* chance is a fault in plot-construction; it mars many of Plautus's plays, for instance.

But the plot will not be funny simply because it is constructed in one of these four ways; to be so it will have to involve the absurd. An opinion is absurd when it is contrary to the truth, an action when it is contrary to the correct action. Let us consider how the absurd is involved in the first of these cases, the fool failing. Everyone knows that smoke does not talk or make any sound. The proposition "Smoke talks and makes noises" is not funny; it is simply a false proposition. But anyone who happens to believe it, or to believe that anyone else could believe it, is a fool. In Aristophanes' *Wasps* there is a scene in which the old man—whom his son had shut up in the house to keep him from indulging his mania for serving on juries—tries to escape by the chimney. He makes a noise and is heard and challenged; to put his guards off, he says: "I'm smoke coming out." What is funny here? Not simply his self-betrayal, the frustration of his own intent, but the stupidity of supposing that a patent impossibility would deceive anyone. Precisely the same form of a stupidly self-defeating act is the basis of many jokes. Chickens do not talk, any more than smoke does; but you remember the chicken-thief surprised in the hen-house. "Who's there?" "Nobody here but us chickens, mister." Or Ole Olesson hiding from the sheriff in a bag marked CHAINS; when the sheriff kicks the bag, Ole, remembering his disguise, says "Yingle, yingle." In all of these cases the act is contrary to the right thing to do, and it produces a result contrary to the one intended.

But the fool sometimes succeeds by happy chance.

Teacher: Name something used to conduct electricity. Student: Why, er—. Teacher: That's right, wire. Now name a unit of measure of electricity. Student: What? Teacher: That's right, watt. This is a peculiarly dismal joke, but it is the shortest I could think of. As matter of fact many excellent jokes and scenes in comedy involve this business of the right act done by accident, or the wrong act accidentally producing the right result. Do you remember Harpo Marx in one of his movies? He had a passion for playing slot-machines or anything that resembled them in the least, so he put coins into telephone coinboxes and streetcar conductors' change-holders and vending machines and always hit the jackpot. The lucky fool is an important figure in comedy.

The clever act, or sometimes merely the sensible act, can also fail by accident. In *The Frogs*, for example, Dionysius has disguised himself as Herakles for his journey into the underworld, hoping that all the friends Herakles made on his trip will mistake him for Herakles and treat him well. But then he meets Aeacus, who berates the supposed hero for stealing his dog Cerberus, and who threatens him with all sorts of horrors. In fear of Aeacus, Dionysius makes his slave change costumes with him; whereupon the new Herakles is invited to a banquet. Dionysius makes his slave exchange costumes again, whereupon the landlady of an inn accuses him of having skipped without paying his enormous bill. They change costumes once again, and Dionysius finds himself in fresh difficulty. Here we have a series of perfectly sensible acts which produce the wrong consequences. You may remember W. C. Fields, as a policeman, coming up to a man leaning against a building: "What do you think you're doing, holding up the building? Move on." The man does, and the building falls.

The success of the ordinarily sensible act is not comic, but the success of the clever act may be. The clever act is as remote from the ordinary as the stupid or foolish one is; the fool does something obviously wrong, the clever man something inobviously right; he achieves the apparently impossible or difficult by apparently impossible, or at any rate inobvious, means. Cleverness in itself is not comic, although it is always pleasing; it becomes comic only when it makes someone look ridiculous (particularly if that person has been trying to ridicule the clever man) or when the act performed is apparently, but not really, absurd, or when it produces a comic reversal. Sganarelle in *The Flying Doctor* is a good example; his quick wit saves him from exposure again and again.

If the absurd in matters of intellect is what is most counter to the true, and in matters of action what is most counter to the practical, evidently every one of these four kinds entails a real or apparent absurdity; acts of folly will always be absurd, and in the case of the lucky fool there will be a further absurdity in the relation of act to result; acts of cleverness will, in their inobviousness and apparent extravagance, as I have explained, *seem* absurd, and in the case of the unlucky clever man entail real absurdity in the relation of act to result. We must note that the two terms in an absurdity —for instance, "smoke" and "talking" in our example from *The Wasps*—may be a neutral combination, or they may cause pleasure or displeasure from their combination, over and above that resulting from the absurdity itself; they may constitute something, as we say, "pleasant or unpleasant to think of." Thus the waltzing lion in Shaw's *Androcles and the Lion*, together with many of the charming absurdities in the plays of Giraudoux, are pleasant, while the absurdities in what are called "sick" jokes are unpleasant. You remember the Little Audrey jokes:

LITTLE AUDREY: But Mother I don't want to go to Europe.
MOTHER: Shut up and keep on swimming.

or

LITTLE AUDREY: But Mother I don't like baby brother.
MOTHER: Shut up and eat what's put before you.

Sick humor has often been thought peculiarly characteristic of our age; but our parents laughed at things like

> Willy, in one of his brand-new sashes,
> Fell in the fire and was burned to ashes;
> By and by the room grew chilly
> But no one wanted to poke up Willy.

We have been talking all along about comic success and failure. In the serious forms this is a matter of happiness and misery, and in tragedy, thus, pity and fear are aroused; pity, as Aristotle says, for undeserved misfortune, fear for the man like ourselves. The extremer forms of comedy reverse this; as we have seen, the ridiculous figure, insofar as he is ridiculous, is *unlike* us, and therefore not someone for whom we feel fear; and the misfortune is not undeserved. But also it is nothing very great; for then we should be back in the serious again. I have already observed that comedy may deal with murder, rape, incest, tortures, deaths, illnesses, crimes of all sorts; and as a matter of fact these are far more frequent in comedy than in tragedy. For instance, in Menander's *Epitrepontes*—translated title, *The Arbitration*—we have the rape of a young girl, the exposure of a child, extreme marital unhappiness, desertion, etc.; crucifixion threatens in Plautus' or in Terence's plays every now and then; read outlines of the plays of Plautus and Terence and you will imagine that you are reading serious stories that end happily. Comedy, then, debars no subject matter as such, and hence no misfortune as such. What it does is to take a lighthearted view of such things; we saw in our first chapter that it did so by establishing causes *contrary* to those that would produce a grave or serious view. Usually, of course, the ultimate misfortune in comedy amounts to no more than embarrassment or humiliation where the characters are capable of shame, or where they are not, chagrin, failure of plans, discomfiture, loss of money, power, or nothing more than a good beating. If there is severer punishment, it is either passed over lightly or rendered absurd. Comparably, final good fortune usually amounts to marriage, the reconciliation of friends and families, the gain of money or office, rescue from an embarrassment, etc. If comedy relaxes concern by exhibiting its grounds as absurd, it is most effectively comic when it treats of things which do arouse our concern.

We have now, I hope, a fairly clear view of the most elementary forms of comic plot, in terms of who does what with what result. Out of these, all others are generated in one or both of two ways: first, by what I shall call mechanical development, and, second, by what I shall call qualitative development.

By "mechanical development" I mean the working out of different ways in which these elementary acts can be combined into different structures or patterns, quite apart from any other considerations. For example, the most obvious thing we can do with them is to string them together in a series. The series may be a set of acts completely unrelated except that the same agent performs them. This is not much of a plot, but there are such constructions. Or the series can be given more unity by having all the actions involve the same situation. Some vaudeville skits have only such unity. Again, the act can simply be repeated a number of times. If you do this, you will have a pattern plot. Thornton

Wilder's *The Queens of France* has a pattern plot; in it you
see a man swindle three different women, each of whom he
has led to believe that she is the Queen of France. *Pippa
Passes* is another example; so is Schnitzler's *Reigen* or *La
Ronde*, except that here the agents change. Again, you can
have the acts successively related as cause and effect, so that
A produces B, B produces C, and so on. You will now have a
consecutive plot. Such a plot will still not be a whole, because
you can go on indefinitely in that fashion, always adding
more acts. If you want it to be a whole and complete as a
series, you will have to give it a definite beginning and end.
The simplest way to do this is to make all the constituent
acts part of one single act. For example, in Molière's Don
Juan play, *Le Festin de pierre*, Don Juan gets rid of his creditor Monsieur Dimanche by professing such warm friendship
and showing such solicitude for him that the creditor never
gets to demand his money. That is one single act; but it is
made up of many constituent acts, all similar to the envelop-
ing larger act. Again, you can build out of dissimilar acts
which are related as stages of a single process. You will thus
have what Aristotle calls a simple plot. Put a reversal in it,
so that the series moves first in one direction, then in the
contrary—say, first toward misfortune, then toward good fortune—and you will have a complex plot. Again, moving away
from consecutive plots, you can put the incidents together
so that altogether they amount to a description of something
—say, a journey, as in Wilder's *The Happy Journey from
Trenton to Camden*, or of a typical day of someone, or of a
man walking his dog, as in Marcel Marceau's little sketch.
You will now have a descriptive plot. Again, you can fit the
incidents together so that they form premises from which an
inference must be gathered; this is a didactic plot, and the
plots of all thesis-plays are so constructed.

All this is simply supposing a single agent, with all other characters passive, so that only a single line of action results. But you can have two or more agents, and correspondingly many more lines of action; and these can be differently inter-related. You can have two or more agents operating unwittingly at cross-purposes, so that they frustrate each other's purposes until they discover what is happening. Or you can have them in conflict, until the conflict ends in victory for one or a compromise or whatever. Or you can have them simply contrast with one another or resemble one another; a very common form of this in comedy is one line operating as a parody of another. Indeed, you have this even in serious plays: in Marlowe's *Doctor Faustus* the Wagner episodes parody the actions of Faustus. One line can be principal and the others subordinate, moreover, or you can have all coordinate. Finally, you can interweave two or more complete stories in the same fashion. This is what the Romans called *contaminatio;* it was supposedly invented by Gnaeus Naevius, and Terence employs it—for instance, his *Andria* is a conflation of the *Perinthia* and the *Andria* of Menander, and his *Eunuch* is a conflation of Menander's *The Eunuch* and *The Flatterer*. And the stories can of course be contrasting or similar. And one can be used as a kind of frame for the other, as in Shaw's *Fanny's First Play* and all plays within plays, and sometimes the framing action is the more important—for instance, the general action in *A Midsummer Night's Dream* is more important than the Pyramus and Thisbe play—or the less important like the Christopher Sly episodes in *The Taming of the Shrew*. Finally, comic plots may have a double issue—that is, good fortune for one, bad for the other—or a single; whereas tragic plots are most effective with a single issue.

This is enough to give you some idea of the vast number

of structures we can build out of our simple little bricks by what I called mechanical development; but we must also consider qualitative development. By this I mean whatever gives the plot as a whole its comic quality, and its peculiar kind of comic quality. As I said last time, the comic plot need not consist wholly of comic incidents; it is comic if the overall action is comic. For instance, if the plot is one long process, it is comic if the process is, not because all phases of the process are.

What the comic is in general I expounded in the preceding chapters. I defined it as something that produced a relaxation of concern by exhibiting an apparent absurdity in the grounds of concern, and I stated that the comic response depended on three conditions: to state it in terms of laughter (though you remember it was not necessarily a matter of laughter), (1) the kind of person laughed at, (2) the frame of mind of the laugher, and (3) the particular cause of the laughter, all of which I analyzed at length. The problem, I think, is insoluble except in terms of these conditions, for otherwise, as I showed, we get into the endless business of asking about what a Hottentot or an Eskimo laughs at, and so on. Now it involves the absurd, and, as I argued, the absurd is seen only by comparison with a standard. And standards vary, for they are opinions of what is right and proper in any given instance, and such opinions vary with the class and education, intelligence and character and so on, of the people who hold them. Again, a judgment is reached by means of the standard, i.e., a judgment that the thing is absurd, and such judgments may be right or wrong: something may be judged as absurd when it is not. And there are different standards, too, of what should or should not be laughed at, for brutal persons may laugh at a man who is being led to execution, or at the commission of some great crime. Of course we judge these standards themselves; and so we get such classifications of humor as gross or refined, brutal or humane, intelligent or stupid or silly, or the like. Thus this joke is revolting, while that one is stupid, and another is clever; and we are talking about comic quality. These are clearly moral distinctions; they are very relevant indeed; but they cannot be made by artistic principles, for they belong to ethics; art rather assumes them, bases on them, does not establish them.

Again, the comic quality is dependent upon the relation of the one who laughs to the one he laughs at. That relation is either friendly or hostile or indifferent. The comic quality of Fielding's *Tom Jones*, for example, is very different from that of his *Jonathan Wild;* the narrator in the one is fond of Tom and indulgent toward most of his faults, the narrator in the other detests Jonathan Wild. People are glad to see the worth of their enemies belittled; that is why they insult and slight them if they can; but among friends the worth of the person is taken as beyond question, in which case ridicule is actually praise ironically expressed, or the fault is considered unimportant (this is the opposite of damning with faint praise); or the person is not wholly good but likely to be, and at any rate better than most (this is *Tom Jones*); or else the whole thing is mere play; you have doubtless seen many close friends exchange mock-insults as a sort of game. Comedy seems to have begun with personal insult and invective; as it developed, it moved from the particular to the universal, that is, to *kinds* of ridiculous people quite apart from personal feeling, and it only then became true comedy. Anger and hatred are serious emotions, and expel the comic emotion. Still, we enjoy malicious wit when the victim seems to deserve it; and accordingly we must say that comic quality can also vary from the hostile to the friendly; only we must be made to feel that the object deserves whatever he gets.

Finally, the comic quality varies with the kind of probability entailed in the action. It makes a great deal of difference in our comic response whether the incidents are necessary or probable as such (this is the only kind of probability that Aristotle is chiefly concerned with), or necessary or probable only when understood as exaggerations, or so only once we have assumed a given hypothesis. We have, thus, at least three kinds of probability: one based on the *natural* (that is, what a given kind of man will really do or say), another which we may call *hyperbolical*, since it is based upon hyperbole, and another which we may call *hypothetical*, since it is based upon a hypothesis. Thus we have comedies in which things happen much as they do in life; and we have comedies in which there is probability of exaggeration—farce and burlesque are of this sort; and comedies which require you to accept a certain impossible assumption, as in fantasies and things of the sort. You all know comedies of these kinds, and you know that you respond differently to them. There is a great difference, for instance, between your responses to *The Taming of the Shrew*, Shaw's *The Music-Cure*, and Giraudoux's *Ondine*.

Needless to say, perhaps: the comic quality of the play is the comic quality of the *whole* action—the action as a whole —rather than that of particular parts. For example, the waltzing lion bit in Shaw is farce, but the whole play is not. Nor is the whole action of *A Midsummer Night's Dream* of the same comic quality as the Pyramus and Thisbe play, or the episodes involving Bottom and Titania.

Well: you see we have cast our great dialectical nets far and wide; if you look carefully, I think you will see the comic for the Borneo caveman and the Hottentot and who not, wriggling somewhere among our catch; and everything from what arouses boisterous laughter to what merely brings a twinkle to the eye. (It was because I wanted such big nets, by the way, that I refused to confine the comic to laughter.)

We must now deal rapidly and briefly with other matters. First, just a word or two more about comic character. I have already said that the primarily comic is always about people, and about all else secondarily and only by analogy or some other relation to people; I have also said that people are comic through appearance, which includes facial expression, dress, motions, etc. (which in drama are rather matters for the director, costumier, and make-up man); comic through their acts, a question we have fully examined; they are also comic, however, in virtue of their emotions, desires, and dispositions, and in addition, their speech. Take emotion, merely as an example, and run it through the Aristotelian categories; it is comic when it is the wrong emotion (e.g., someone is frightened when there is no cause), or there is too much or too little of it (quantity), or it is of the wrong quality (e.g., *royal* emotion in a clown), or related to the wrong thing, e.g., anger at the wrong man or at the wrong place or time, etc.; and to be comic, as we know, it must be absurdly wrong. Insofar as we mean character as a *part* of comedy, the same conditions apply as in tragedy: the character should be useful to the plot, have the traits appropriate to him as an agent, etc.

Comic *diction* is a very large subject: let me see if I can put it in a nutshell. First, there are two kinds, according to our distinction between butt and wit: the one who makes himself comic through speech, and the one who makes others comic. People make themselves ridiculous by speech through some absurd fault: of enunciation, or dialect, or grammatical errors, or being too prolix or concise, or by employing the wrong style (e.g., bombast about trivial or low things), or by accidentally revealing their true feelings or otherwise doing the opposite of their intent—e.g., insulting while trying to compliment, boasting but revealing the absurdity of the boast, etc. Such comic diction is not produced, as many theorists have thought, by the use of certain tropes and figures, but by the absurd *misuse* of any trope or figure whatsoever. In a word, it is either faulty in itself or reveals some fault, in the comic way.

The comic diction of the wit, on the other hand, may involve all the resources of rhetoric insofar as they suit his purpose, his character, and the occasion. Wit ranges from the obvious to the subtle. Obvious wit states; subtle wit implies; obvious wit is concerned with the superficial; subtle wit sees more deeply. Innuendo, irony, metaphor, and comparison all involve inference; the more stages of inference involved— that is, the more syllogisms requisite to get at what is implied —the subtler the wit. Diction also permits of suspense and surprise; and surprise after long anticipation will increase the effect.

The diction of wit and butt are in a respect contrary to each other. The diction of the butt is appropriate if it is *inappropriate* in the required way; the diction of the wit, simply appropriate.

CHAPTER IV

Aristophanes, Plautus, Terence

Among the important problems still unsettled in the theory of comedy are those of the principles by which the kinds of comedy should be distinguished, and the kinds that would thus result. Indeed, many will not admit that such problems are important; people who would reject any simple division of the animal or vegetable kingdom often dismiss the problem of classification in drama by quoting Polonius' famous classification in *Hamlet* as supposedly the worst of pedantries. Those who do find some interest in classifying proceed on a mass of conflicting principles: some according to the comic quality—high comedy, low comedy, sentimental comedy, etc.; others according to subject matter—comedy of manners, comedy of wit, domestic comedy; still others according to the kind of probability entailed—fantastic, realistic, etc.; while still others classify by techniques or conventions, to go no further.

If you ask me why I think we should worry about species, I will respond that I find it quite evident that what is successful in one kind may well bring failure in another, that a good judge of one is not necessarily a good judge of another, that a writer may have a gift for one but not for the other, and that this suggests that we have here a number of distinct arts, all grouped together under one general art. If that is true, it is important to distinguish kinds and thus important to distinguish them correctly.

In that case, on what principles ought species of comedy to be distinguished? Surely, if plot is most important—we have assumed that, and Aristotle proved it—*through the plot*, and surely through what gives the plot its effect. Now the plot is given its effect primarily through reversal and discovery; hence one form is the complex plot. Again, we saw that the good plot in comedy involved comic suffering—beatings, embarrassments, and the like, comparable to scenes of pathos in tragedy. Hence, a second kind is that of comic suffering. Third, since character involves thought and diction, there is possible the kind of character. Music we may dismiss, either as unable of itself to make a plot comic, or as subsumed as an accessory of diction. There remains, then, the comic of spectacle. Four basic kinds, then: the complex, as in all those plays of Plautus and Terence in which the resolution is brought about through the discovery that the slave girl is really a free person, or someone's long lost sister, as well as all plays of discovered deception, like *Volpone;* the play of comic suffering, as in Molière's *The Jealousy of Barbouillé*, his *The Imaginary Cuckold* and *The Forced Marriage;* the play of character, like *The Taming of the Shrew;* and finally, the play of spectacle, like the plays of Gozzi's which depend almost wholly on transformations. The fertility of dramatic invention is such that dramatists "multiply variety" in a bewildering fashion; but they reduce, I believe, to these four basic kinds.

The only other *essential* distinction is that relating to the comic quality itself, as high or low; and of this, as I have said before, the *eutrapelos*, the man of well-turned wit, is the standard.

It is a good idea, when examining plots, to consider

four things: what sort of incidents make up a plot, and whether these are possible, probable, or impossible in themselves, either generally or in the given circumstances, as well as what emotional quality they have; (2) what binding principle ties the incidents together, whether consequential probability or something else; (3) what shape or configuration of plot results; (4) to what end the whole is addressed, whether pleasure, or something over and above pleasure.

Suppose we look at Aristophanes in these terms. We may begin by considering the following crude account of part of what happens in a certain play (not by Aristophanes):

A young girl is violated by a drunken young man at a carnival. Months later she marries; in her husband's absence she gives birth to a son, whom she exposes in the ancient fashion of dealing with unwanted offspring. Her husband, learning of the child, is furious and goes off to live with a harp-girl. But the wife refuses to divorce him, despite her father's urgings, because she loves him.

Compare that with the following:

An Athenian who wants to put an end to the Peloponnesian War decides to visit the gods and ask their help. He tries first with ladders, but these fail and he cracks his head. He decides to fly, therefore, on the back of a monstrous dung-beetle. Arriving at Zeus's door, he is met by Hermes, who tells him that in disgust with the Greeks, the gods have moved away and left War and Tumult to rule in their stead. War enters and begins to make a salad, the first step in the preparation of which involves grinding up all the Greek cities with a pestle. Having just moved in, he has no pestle; so he sends his slave Tumult to borrow one from Athens or from Sparta. But Athens and Sparta have lost their pestles, so War goes out to get one.

Now I think you will agree that in the first example

every single incident was perfectly possible; indeed, given the times and customs, rather more than that; and the whole string of consequences, given the first incident, is perfectly probable. I do not think you can claim that for the second. If we take it literally, it recounts almost sheer nonsense. It is possible that someone should ask the gods for help; it is not possible to visit them, unless you accept myths. If it were possible, it would not be possible with ladders, and certainly not on the back of a dung-beetle, even if dung-beetles came in the right size. If I recounted the first example to you as something that had really happened in antiquity, you would have accepted it without question. If I recounted the second as real events which happened in antiquity or any other time, you would begin to entertain some suspicion of me. Well, but it really did happen; not all of it, perhaps, and not precisely in that way; but it really happened, and, by the way, War managed to finish that salad. He finished it, to be precise, in 404 b.c., and you may look in your histories and verify the date. There is really nothing strange here; you see things of this sort in your daily newspaper. You see Mao Tse-tung and Kosygin jumping up and down on a piece of white paper, meanwhile quarreling bitterly. Or you see a statue weeping. Or you see a bearded brutal-looking giant in armor about to take a bite out of the world as if it were an apple while a man sits by on a cloud and watches. Sometimes these things are funny, sometimes sobering; but you do not question them, for the white paper is labeled "U.S.-Vietnam White Paper," the statue is the statue of Lincoln—I refer to Mauldin's great cartoon on the assassination of John F. Kennedy—and the bearded giant is labeled War. For you know very well that these are political cartoons.

Precisely, cartoons: and Aristophanes' plays are cartoons in dramatic action. They are a great deal more; but *that* they certainly are. Consider War and his salad; it is completely puzzling if you take it at face value; but if you know that War is the Peloponnesian War, which began in 431 B.C., that among the ingredients which he intends to braise are leeks (standing for Prasiae in Laconia), cheese (meaning Sicily), onions (meaning Megara), and honey (meaning Athens), and that consequently making the salad means destroying all Greece; that his being without a pestle means that he has no man at the moment he can use to crush Greece, and that the loss of the Athenian pestle means the death of the Athenian demagogue Cleon and the loss of the Spartan pestle means the death of Brasidas, and that War's going to get a pestle means—well, enough of that; if you know all this, the puzzling as impossible becomes the intelligible as actual. What is going on is funny, but it is also puzzling; and you puzzle until you get the point; and then it is funnier still.

This is a technique of *forced identification:* you must identify the things and persons depicted in order to interpret; but when you have interpreted the action you have had to find the likeness of A which you take seriously to a comic B which seems as unlike it as possible; you have had to say, "That's Cleon, that's Brasidas, that's all they were, pestles of war to grind up Greece." You can identify only by finding likenesses in such cases; and you yourself have found the likeness and drawn the inference, so that you have accepted, in imagination at least, the destruction of the claims to value of these men, their causes, and the war. This is very much like metaphor, except that metaphor involves the substitution of words; indeed, the moment you state the action *literally*—as I just did—you get a succession of metaphors for what is really meant. If writers use ordinary words for things, only minimum interpretation is required: *The cat is on the mat,* for instance, is not too difficult to interpret. The moment metaphor is introduced, however, further interpretation is required, for you have to find the likeness; this becomes harder as the metaphors are novel and remote, for the likenesses are harder to find; and if you state something *wholly* in metaphors of this kind you will have a riddle. "The five-legged spider seized its brazen prey and drew the wooden leaf that makes a vacancy"; you will have to do a little work on that to find out that it means "The hand grasped the door knob and pulled it open." Even then you will not be quite sure. Because of that uncertainty, that shattering obscurity, writers have often made use of metaphor to attack things they would not have dared to attack openly.

Aristophanes by no means uses his dramatic metaphors for veiled attack; rather he makes use of the power that metaphors have to dignify or degrade, to make things seem beautiful or ugly, possible or impossible, serious or comic. Think of Homer's "rosy-fingered Dawn"; now think of "red-handed Dawn" or "carrot-fingered Dawn." The curious thing about metaphor is that the mind, once it has grasped the likeness of part to part, tends temporarily at least to identify whole with whole; "rosy-fingered" makes Dawn a maiden, "carrot-fingered" a serving wench; so that Cleon and Brasidas become pestles and nothing more.

Now, if you want to make dramatic cartoons like those of Aristophanes, you will have to find metaphors which are visual or auditory, and ones that involve actions that can be depicted on the stage. And they will have to be ridiculous—extravagantly so: you can do this by choosing metaphors which debase as much as possible (a kind of inverted hyperbole) without arousing disgust or any serious emotion, and by including the absurd. You must debase and make absurd everything but the likeness which relates the metaphor to the thing you mean; for if you alter that, your whole stratagem fails; instead of hitting your target, you make your use of the metaphor itself absurd.

We can see something of how this operates if we consider another favorite device of Aristophanes: parody. The dung-beetle flight to the gods in *Peace* is funny simply as such; but it becomes much funnier if you happen to know that it is a parody of the tragedy *Bellerophon* by one of Aristophanes' favorite victims, Euripides. We possess only fragments of this play, but we know enough about it to say that in it Bellerophon, mounted on Pegasus, flew to Heaven to remonstrate with the gods; that he prayed for safety on this perilous flight, and that he described the view below him as he rose. Look how Aristophanes subverts all this. A horse is a noble animal; a winged horse must be much nobler, and Pegasus must be noblest of all; he is replaced by a dung-beetle, and an extravagantly large and voracious one at that. Bellerophon is a mythical hero; he is replaced by Trygaeus, an Athenian farmer. The flight—possible to a mythical hero, impossible here—also involves a description of the view, which includes a man doing something that threatens to divert the dung-beetle from his course. The flight also has its perils: Trygaeus prays to the gods—but also to the stage-hands to give him a safe flight.

Sometimes a substantial portion of the action is parody; *The Frogs* for instance, is in great part a parody of Herakles' journey to the underworld, and this too perhaps is a hit at Euripides' *Hercules Furens*. Herakles the brave hero is replaced by the god Dionysius *dressed* as Herakles. He is cowardly in Euripides' play to the point where he twice, through fear, has what mothers call "an accident." Herakles had gone to the underworld to bring back Theseus King of Athens; the mock-Herakles goes to bring back Euripides. Herakles had performed the heroic exploit of bringing back with him also the terrible dog-monster Cerberus; the *mock*-Herakles is denounced as a dog-thief.

It is never parody which creates the overall form for Aristophanes, however. In fact, the matter of overall form is controversial, for Aristophanes' ability in dramatic construction has often been questioned. Gilbert Norwood, for example, denies that he is a great playwright and remarks:

> He could indeed conceive and carry through gloriously clever and amusing situations; but . . . we must recognize that the structure of his dramas is on the whole loose and faltering. . . . If we refuse to be blinded by his reputation, we may easily see how these plays were composed . . . [he] conceived a splendid comic idea and then wrote ahead, dashing off lyrics and scenes just as they occurred to him. . . .[1]

Now this is somewhat plausible as a judgment *if* you assume with Professor Norwood that there is only one kind of plot: the kind that, in the preceding chapter, I called the extended consecutive plot, the only kind which Aristotle considers. Such a kind, whether tragic or comic, has as its end the pleasure which results from the play of the aroused emotions. But it is also possible that the pleasure itself, instead of being final, may be used as means to a further end; and that alters the matter greatly. Aristophanes does not *fail* to make consecutive plots; he does not *try* to make them. What he does do is to use dramatic action as an instrument of persuasion—that is, it is the rhetorical possibilities of comedy, *not* the poetic, which interest him. He himself repeatedly says as much.

Indeed, it may be said that every one of the extant eleven plays except the *Thesmophoriazuae* is comic "proof" of a single main statement; and it is this unity of statement that gives unity to the action, not the consecution of cause and effect.

How can you find this statement? Very simple; all you have to do is to ask yourself what the overall action, which will also be a dramatic metaphor, is a metaphor *of*. If you can solve the puzzle of War's salad-making, you can solve the metaphor of the whole action, too, for the same principle is involved. The underlying statement will sometimes be an ironic one, but it will be something about which Aristophanes is very serious—indeed, it may be the only thing in the play about which he is serious. There is no reason to doubt the sincerity of his desire for peace, or the sincerity of his hatred for Cleon or for sophistry and other forces that he thought were undermining his society and state (Euripides among them).

Each of these statements seems to divide into three parts: a supposed desire, a recommended course of action (ironic) as the condition of its fulfillment, and a reason why this is so. "If you want . . . then you must . . . because." Think of the plays: *The Acharnians:* If you want to enjoy the blessings of peace, then you will have to make a private truce, for heaven knows your leaders won't make one. *The Knights:* If you want a leader like Cleon, you ought to choose an even more ill-qualified rascal, for all you want is someone to cater to your weaknesses. *The Clouds:* If you want to avoid your just debts, take up sophistry, for it will turn against you very nicely. *Peace:* If you want the blessings of peace, you must go to heaven and bring her back yourself, for the gods are disgusted with you and won't help you. *Lysistrata:* If you want peace, the only way to get it is for the women to go on a sex-strike; for sex seems to be the only thing the Greeks really care about. And so on.

It is the second of these elements—the ironically recommended course of action—which forms the center of each comedy: making a private truce, choosing a greater rascal, taking up sophistry, going to heaven for peace, going on a sex-strike, bringing back a poet from the dead, building cloud-cuckoo-town, giving up jury-service for Cleon and his gang, having women govern the state, distributing wealth according to merit. Each of these is the basic dramatic metaphor for what Aristophanes really means. The plot falls into two parts: the action expressed by the comic metaphor, and its result. In one instance (*The Acharnians*) the action is complete before the first parabasis (the direct address of the chorus to the audience); sometimes it ends before the second parabasis; the rest of the play is given over to the result.

Along with all this, as you know, there are jokes, charming lyrics, and a great deal of incidental satire, all assisting in the comic effect. I have talked of comic pathos, comic suffering; Aristophanes is a great master of it. The suffering of Lamachus in *The Acharnians*, of Strepsiades in *The Clouds*, of Philocleon in *The Wasps*, of Cinesias in *Lysistrata*, of Dionysius and Xanthias in the flogging scene of *The Frogs*—to name no more—are all remarkable instances.

The quantitative parts, or *conventional format*, of the play in Old Comedy consisted of the prologue, in which, in Aristophanes at least, the protagonist always expounds his intention; the parodos, or entrance of the chorus; the agon, or debate over the intention; the parabasis, or direct address of the chorus to the audience; the episodes, which work out the action; the stasimon or choral song; and the exodos, or concluding song or speech of the chorus as it makes its exit. There is nothing very strict about this; some plays—*The Knights* and *The Clouds*, for example—have a second agon, some—like the two just mentioned—have a second parabasis. Except for the parabasis and the agon, the analogy to the parts of Greek tragedy is striking; possibly comedy modeled upon it.

As comedy developed, the role of the chorus gradually weakened, it ceased to participate in the action, and the parabasis fell into disuse; the prologue took over some of its functions; ultimately the whole format changed. The farcical and satiric elements were replaced in Middle and New Comedy by moralizing and character-study; and the plots, it has often been said, owed much to Euripides. They were plots based upon natural probability, dealing with love-escapades, the separation and reunion of families (the last usually through a recognition by tokens or a last-minute witness), strife and reconciliation, and the like.

E. F. Watling has put this as concisely as anyone I know:

When, with the loss of political belligerence and intellectual freedom, Athens lost the robust virility of Aristophanic comedy, her dramatists discovered in due course . . . the charm of lightly amusing narratives in dramatic form, comfortably reassuring tales of misfortunes mended by kindly providence, quarrels amicably settled . . . lost children . . . restored . . . the course of true love threatened . . . but finally guided into safe harbour.[2]

The bit of summary I gave earlier from Menander's *The Arbitration* is quite typical. Comedy had changed into the comedy of manners. I shall not speak of Menander himself; we have one complete play of his, discovered in the 1950's, plus several more or less substantial fragments, but this seems hardly enough to warrant discussion of his practice. Instead let us consider Plautus and Terence, both of whom composed plays adapted from Greek originals.

The first thing we observe when we look at these writers, from the point of view I have set before you, is that if comedy has expanded, in the sense of venturing into new forms, the *area* of the comic has shrunk. The Aristophanic plots, we say, involved preposterous impossibilities even in their most general statement, and could not be taken seriously at all. But the Plautine and Terentian plots, given general statement, sound no more impossible, and no less serious, than those of Menander. Now, when an action as generally described is plausible and serious, it can become comic only through specification; and such specification is possible only through what I called, in my first chapter, the circumstances of the act: agent, act, object, instrument, purpose, result, manner, time, place; and it is consequently to such circumstantial specification that we must look in order to see the comic aspects of their plots. This can be done with some precision if we can see, in contrast with the general account, the particular specifications and their effects.

Space permits me to do this only illustratively. Consider Plautus' *Rudens, The Rope*. It involves several situations and actions which are of some seriousness. A young girl has been stolen as a child and sold to a procurer. A young man who falls in love with her agrees to buy her and makes a deposit. The procurer absconds with her to Sicily instead, where he expects greater profits, and a violent storm wrecks the ship. The girl and her friend survive, but so do the procurer and his friend. The girls take sanctuary in the temple of Venus, and the priestess befriends them; but the procurer and his friend discover them and seek to wrest them away. They are prevented from doing this by a farmer who takes the girls under his protection. A trunk containing tokens identifying the girl as the farmer's daughter is fished from the sea by a slave, and all ends happily, especially since the girl's true love is on the scene.

Now suppose that you wanted to make this a serious drama: what would you do? The first thing you would do would be to deal with this in terms of developing fear and pathos. This is the kind of thing Shakespeare does so wonderfully in *Othello*. And you would do this by selecting the most fearful and piteous things in the action; thus center everything on the plight of the two girls. The greater stature you could give the heroine, the closer you would come to tragedy; in this case, pathetic tragedy.

On the other hand, if you wanted to make this as comic as possible, given the general probability of the incidents, you would make the characters as *unlike* you as possible, and their misfortunes as *unlike* any that might befall you, and make it unlikely that they would befall even the persons involved. Much has been made of Brecht's theory of the Verfremdungsaffekt, or alienation effect, but it is merely a modified form of comic alienation. The point is that the extreme comic is produced by making the observer so indifferent to the fortunes of the persons he is observing that he can concentrate on the absurdities of action and fortune as such, without emotional commitment.

Now, Plautus does not go so far as that; but he goes, in his characteristic way, far enough. Were you worried about that innocent young girl in the hands of a foul procurer? Believe it or not, she is still a virgin (by the way, free-born girls in such plight always remain mysteriously virgin, by a special convention of the Roman drama). Cruelly treated? Well, no, not really; no real evidence of that. A storm wrecks the ship? Yes; but it was done by Arcturus in order to help her. But her love? The lovers never meet in the play. Surely the recognition by her father must contain some true elements of sentiment? Not at all; he is rebuked for talking like someone in a comedy. All elements of romance, and some of those of melodrama, are shifted far from the center of the play; the characters who are involved in them become *situational characters* (that is, characters constituting a situation for someone else who is principal) rather than anything else. The shift involves dramatic focus: the characters who are *in* focus are not those involved, except indirectly, in anything very serious. On the contrary, their actions are comic, and some very funny indeed.

Consider, too, the *Miles Gloriosus—The Braggart Warrior.* In this a young lover wishes to rescue his beloved from a soldier who has her in his possession. Now every conceivable danger in this play hangs upon the soldier and what he might do to the girl or her lover if he discovered what was up. To make the play serious, that soldier must be made as dangerous as possible. What does Plautus do with him? Two things: he reduces him to a situational character and makes him as such an emptily-bragging coward—the merest caricature of one at that; in short, a ridiculous figure. Duckworth calls him the central figure, which amazes me; he exists only as the object of a ridiculous trick, along with his helper who is also the object of ridiculous tricks; the whole action consists in the tricks themselves. Moreover, he discovers the trick only at the end, too late. And the girl is an extremely adroit and clever girl, abetted by other clever people. The soldier never really has a chance; the suspense lies in the smooth operation of an intricate machine of intrigue.

With plots that involve a serious element, then, Plautus clearly does three things: he neutralizes any potentially pathetic or horrific parts, except when these are at the beginning of the play, as in Palaestra's speech in Act I sc. iii of *The Rope;* he centers upon the line of comic mistake or comic deception, and makes the serious characters situational (an instance is *Casina:* the story is about a dastardly intrigue to possess a young girl, but you never see her—all you see is intrigue and counter-intrigue); he utilizes characters unlikely to fulfill their evil intentions, and characters likely to fulfill their good ones.

I have been speaking of plots which might have involved

some elements of the serious; but Plautus also has plots, like that of *The Menaechmi*, which are pure fun, or, like the *Amphitryon*, almost so. In these his chief problem is to pile consequence upon consequence; in these, too, and in any others, for that matter, he will usually choose a less probable but funnier consequence over a more probable but less funny one. This has given him a name as a careless plot-maker, among those who feel that plot is primarily a construction of probabilities; my own feeling is that it is better to be funny than logical if you are a comedian. In the same fashion he sometimes does not trouble to tie together all the threads of action at the end; but here again his comic purpose is primary for him, and he will drop something that has no evident comic possibilities, or that would require too much additional development to be comic. Resolution is sometimes effected through a husband's or wife's or father's relenting or yielding for no reason that flows from plot, it is true; but I think that sometimes critics mistake the true action of the piece. *Casina*, for example, physically ends with the wife's relenting (she forgives her husband immediately, as she says, only "to keep an already long play from being longer"), and with a perfunctory assurance that Casina will be identified as the long-lost daughter of the man next door and thus be enabled to marry her lover. This seems bad construction, but is not; the true action of the piece is, as I said, the clash of intrigue and counter-intrigue, and the true end is with the discomfiture and exposure of those intriguing against Casina. The girl herself is situational, nearly as impersonal as a deadline that has to be met in a movie about newspapermen.

Plautus' characters, like his situations, tend to fall into a few types: old men, young men, slaves, married women, maids, courtesans, concubines, parasites, soldiers, cooks, usurers. About this there are two extreme views: that expressed in Dryden's *Essay of Dramatic Poesie* by Eugenius, who seems to regard them as stereotypes, and that of E. F. Watling; Watling likens them to the relatively few chess-pieces which can move in an almost infinite number of games. The latter view is more ingenious, but the truth, as so often, seems to lie somewhere in between. On the one hand, if there were *not* a manifest sameness, it would never enter the heads of J. W. Duff and others to defend him from the charge of sameness; on the other, the variety Plautus achieves, given these few elements, is astonishing. If you compared him with the Western movie (or any other genre which also has its stock situations and characters), I think you might be inclined to think that there was far more variety in Plautus; and the way in which these plays have been pillaged or modeled upon to provide new comedies in various literatures over the centuries shows that, few as his elements may have been, they were seminal. Convention seems to have restricted him; yet he works within it to achieve what variety he can. His fathers range from fine old men like Theopropides in *The Haunted House* or Daemones in *The Rope* to the almost base Demaenetus in the *Comedy of Asses* (*Asinaria*) and the even baser Lysidamus in *Casina*. His courtesans range from the loving and kind-hearted Philematium in *The Haunted House* to gold-diggers like Acroteleutium in *The Braggart Warrior* and the basely mercenary and deceitful Phronesium in *Truculentus*. His soldiers range from Stratophanes to Pyrgopolynices; his slaves from devoted ones like Messenio to deceitful ones like Epidicus and Pseudolus. And so on with the rest. Plautus is far from assuming moral character on the basis of class, race, or profession—a point of view that many people still have not achieved.

Even if a dramatist has fully worked out his plot and characters, he still has the problem of the representation or scenario: that is, the plan for what is to be enacted or said by whom in what order. Let me say briefly that what should not be shown on stage and what should, and on what scale (long scene, short scene, etc.) are matters governed by certain principles: those of probability and of emotional effect. If a scene weakens probability or the effect of the action, for instance, it should not be shown, even if it forms an important part of the plot; and conversely, if a scene strengthens probability or effect, it may be well to show it even if it is outside the plot. I state this to make two points: first, if one studies the scenarios of Plautus in these terms, one finds many excellences that have been overlooked. Second—though this is less important—Plautus again and again makes use of the representation to cut out any potential seriousness of the scene; he will, that is, shatter the dramatic illusion to remind his audience that it is only a play they are watching, only a comedy, in fact, and by no means to be taken too seriously. Aristophanes of course shattered the dramatic illusion, too, as in Trygaeus' beseeching the stagehands to give him a safe flight on the dung-beetle; but he is merely adding another dimension of the ridiculous, whereas Plautus is doing something more.

But now we must say a few words about Terence. Like Plautus and Caecilius Statius, he wrote *fabulae palliatae*, plays based on the matter of the Greek New Comedy. He has always been given credit for being a finer technician than Plautus, who has the carelessness of exuberance; at the same time, he fell into mistakes of *art* which Plautus always avoided. This is a somewhat unconventional judgment, so I had better explain it. If the theory of comedy I expounded in my first three chapters is correct, comedy must avoid the base—the really base—as it must avoid the noble. But in *The Eunuch* of Terence, one brother poses as a eunuch to gain access to a young girl. He succeeds, and ravishes her. Now—as you may have gathered—rape was no new thing in the New Comedy, and it is involved in three or four places in Plautus; it is carnival time, the young man is drunk, and whatever else may have seemed to mitigate the act in the eyes of the ancients. But this is a different matter. This was a deliberate plot; the girl resisted bitterly (we are told that her dress was in rags and that her hair was torn out); she felt such grief and shame afterward that she could not speak, but only cry bitterly; the young man tries to brazen it out, fails, is charged with adultery and threatened with the customary punishment—which, by the way, would ensure that he would not commit a second such offense; he is rescued (naturally rejoicing) from his predicament by the discovery that she is a citizen and that her brother is willing to let him marry her. The repellent matters, moreover, are put repeatedly and vividly before us a number of times; we have even the description of the rape by the rapist, who is very pleased with himself. He "would have been a true eunuch had he acted otherwise"; and besides, he has a good excuse: there was a picture of Zeus with Danae in the room, and who was he to resist when Zeus could not? (You may remember this piece of sophistry from Aristophanes' *Clouds*.) Now *that* is a true *mistake of art*, which quite goes beyond any mere matter of improbability: it quite destroys the possibility of the required emotional response. There is another mistake of art in the conclusion: the other brother (they belong to the same breed in more senses than one) agrees to share his beloved with a rich rival, to lessen expenses. Dante put that beloved (she is the courtesan Thais) in his hell, by the way; you will find her among the flatterers (and in very poor condition, to say the least) because of a single remark she made in this play: *Ingentes*, enormously. But almost everyone else who acts in the play belongs in hell; if there is none, it will be necessary to invent one for such people.

Perhaps one might say that Terence's intention here is satiric: to show the repellent as repellent, so that we may know it. If so, he has certainly succeeded, but it was quite unnecessary; this much we know already, if we have any decency in us. Again, the old man toiling at his self-imposed hard labor in *The Self Tormentor*, to no end except to punish himself for having brought about his son's departure, is neither comic nor satiric, but simply painful. For me, at least, it casts a shadow over the whole play, for no good reason as far as I can see. In Plautus' *The Captives*, Tyndarus must suffer in the quarries, but this is necessary for the plot; and he himself jokes about it. But in Terence's case, these and similar incidents seem real failures to remain within comic limits.

Yet this fault, if it is a fault, is perhaps the shadow of one of his greatest virtues; his tendency to humanize the characters. If we may observe a shrinkage in the comic area from Aristophanes to the New Comedy, as I remarked, we may observe a further shrinkage from Plautus to Terence. The comic, I have said, is based on the unlike; as we make the characters more and more like, we limit the comic range. I do not wish to imply that this is a regression in art; for as we set limits in art, we always thereby open fresh areas of exploration within those limits, explorations that would hardly have been possible without the limits themselves. The course of comedy was to move from the incident which was comic because it was preposterous in itself to the incident which was comic because of the characters involved in it. Pyrgopolynices in Plautus' *Braggart Warrior* is sheer caricature; Thraso, vain soldier in Terence's *Eunuch*, is Pyrgopolynices made more human; had there been no Pyrgopolynices, there would have been no Thraso, and had there been no Thraso, there would have been no Falstaff.

Comedy began with the particular—that is, with invective addressed to individuals—and worked its way toward universals, as Aristotle tells us; what he could not have known is that, once it had established its universals, it began dividing these into ever more specific universals until it produced fictitious characters who—while still universal—gave every impression of being individuals. That is, from accusing this particular man of bragging, it worked its way to the braggart as type; then it broke up the types by subdivision, exploring the different kinds of man who brag. This process gave us all the great comic figures, like Falstaff, whom we hardly think of as fictitious at all.

The various points of Terence's technique—his manipulation of the double story, his use of recognition for complication as well as resolution, his refinements of comic style—all these have long been worked out by others and are no doubt well known to you, and so I shall pass over them. But it was Plautus and Terence who were to dominate the comic poets, as Seneca was to dominate the tragic poets, of the Renaissance; Plautus and Terence lived on, thus, not merely in their own works, but in the works of others. In a sense we shall still be speaking of them, therefore, when we discuss some of the great comedies of Shakespeare and Molière.

CHAPTER V

Shakespeare and Molière

One of the difficulties you are bound to run into, if you proceed as I have in this book—that is, by constructing a definition and building upon it—is that sooner or later you are bound to run into things that are given the name but do not fit the definition. Such things always appear as exceptions and may even be used as objections to the definition; and when the thing has borne the name for a long time, the objections seem very authoritative and powerful ones, and may discredit the definition entirely. We ran into several such difficulties, as a matter of fact, in the last chapter, and I either ignored them or touched upon them but lightly. It was not that I wished to gloss over them; it was simply that I did not want to complicate further an already complicated argument.

Now, however, we must candidly face them. There are "comedies" of Shakespeare (and for that matter, of Molière and others) which do not fit the definition we have constructed; they most certainly do not effect a relaxation of concern through the absurd, even with all the latitude we managed to give the term "absurd" in Chapter III. *The Two Gentlemen of Verona, Measure for Measure,* and *The Winter's Tale,* for instance, depict serious actions; so—despite the little trick of the rings that Portia and Nerissa play upon their husbands at the end—does *The Merchant of Venice*. I will not try to save the matter by observing that they involve comic characters and scenes; so, for that matter, do the tragedies supposedly; and I clearly stated, furthermore, that we had to consider not parts but the action as a whole.

The fact is that they belong to a quite different breed. This may be disappointing to you, but it is not damaging to our project. The question is not whether we managed to describe everything that happens to be called by a certain name, but whether we did accurately describe a given definite area of literature; and if that is so, the next question is not whether our definition fits everything called comedy, but whether a given play fits our definition and so is or is not comedy in our sense of the term. And the "comedies" just mentioned are no more really comedies than *Cymbeline* and *Pericles Prince of Tyre*—which are classified as tragedies, and are not tragedies. Indeed, they are all of the same kind.

Nor am I being very original in saying this. Critics at least beginning with Samuel Johnson have said it; and some, like Bradley and Saintsbury and E. K. Chambers, have held that the proper term for them is *romance*. How they came to be called comedies is by no means inexplicable, but it is no part of our concern here. This much is clear: they would require a poetic much different from the one I have been outlining.

Still, perhaps I seem arbitrary; let me try to explain. Consider *Much Ado About Nothing*. Is it a comedy? To answer that question we must look at its plot. It is a double plot; that is, it contains two clearly distinguishable stories, which as a matter of fact do not have much to do with each other, except that they have some characters in common. One is the tale of how Beatrice and Benedick were brought to love each

other through the intriguing of their friends. This is unques-
tionably comic in our sense; and were that the only action,
we should have comedy. But the other story—that of Hero
and Claudio—is a quite different matter. You remember it:
Don John, the bastard brother of the prince of Aragon,
means to shame his brother by showing that he is sponsoring
a scandalous marriage. To do this, he arranges a scene in
which Margaret, posing as Hero, bids Borachio good night
from Hero's window, as if after an assignation, the night before Hero's marriage to Claudio; Claudio and the prince are
brought to witness this. Furious at what he thinks he sees,
Claudio denounces Hero in the church as unchaste, and
breaks off the wedding. Hero swoons, is reported dead; Dog-
berry's comic watchmen overhear a conversation that betrays
the plot; the scandal is shown to be false, the lovers are re-
united. Now such a story *could* be made comic; the point is
that it is not. It is handled with all seriousness, and we take it
seriously. Is it the principal action? I do not think that we
can say that one or the other of these actions is principal, for
neither depends on the other in any way in which a subordinate plot depends upon a principal one. They are two
perfectly independent actions, unconnected except that Beatrice persuades Benedick to challenge Claudio to a duel
(which, incidentally, does not come to pass). It would be
quite possible, indeed, to separate them, without damage to
either, and make two different shorter plays, unconnected
save that they have some characters in common. Were the
story of Hero subordinate to that of Beatrice and Benedick,
we should have comedy; as the case is, however, I should say
we do not, even though we have many comic scenes. The
title of the play is a misnomer; the story of Hero is certainly
not "much ado about nothing."

I should thus eliminate it, along with *The Two Gentle-*

men of Verona, Measure for Measure, All's Well That Ends Well, As You Like It, The Merchant of Venice, Twelfth Night, The Tempest, and *The Winter's Tale*, from the roster of the fourteen so-called comedies in the Shakespeare canon. I hope it is clear that this is not a value-judgment but simply a distinction of kinds; for some of these are obviously very great plays indeed. We are left, then, with only five comedies in our sense of the word: *The Merry Wives of Windsor, The Comedy of Errors, Love's Labour's Lost, A Midsummer Night's Dream*, and *The Taming of the Shrew*.

Why do I call *them* comedies? you may ask. Well, look at their actions. In *Love's Labour's Lost* the young king of Navarre and three companion lords join in a project to study three years together, and swear an oath that they will live for intellect alone during that time, suppressing the demands of the body: they will fast one day a week, and eat only one meal on the other days, sleep only three hours a night, and debar all ladies from their company. Now this last, given their youth and spirit, is an impossible project, as one of them (Biron) in fact insists; they have no sooner sworn than the princess of France comes on a mission, with just the right number of attendant ladies; she must be entertained and all the couples fall in love at first sight; and the young men themselves recognize the absurdity of their plan. In *The Comedy of Errors* we have the same confusion of identities, with absurd consequences, that we had in Plautus' *Menaechmi*, on which it is based; only Shakespeare introduces *two* sets of identical twins, thereby multiplying the possibilities of error, adds Luciana to supply a love-interest, and frames the chief action in the story of Aegeon and Adriana, which is the only serious element in it. *A Midsummer Night's Dream* is also framed in a serious action, the marriage of Theseus and Hippolyta; but the three actions thus enveloped

—the tiff between Oberon and Titania and how it was settled, the plan of Bottom & Co. for a play, and the resolution of the problems of the Athenian lovers—constitute the main action and are obviously comic. Finally, I do not suppose that anyone would advance the claim that *The Merry Wives of Windsor* and *The Taming of the Shrew* depict serious actions; although a certain lady who wrote on Shakespeare was much upset to see, as she put it, a fine proud-spirited girl subjugated by a crass brute to the point where she became the typical Elizabethan slave-wife.

In Chapter IV I distinguished four basic types of comic plot, under two main heads, plots of folly and plots of cleverness, plots of folly being those in which the agent acts in error for whatever reason, and plots of cleverness being those in which the stratagems of the agent produce the comic action. We have four basic types, I argued, because in each of these the agent succeeds or fails according as he has good or bad intentions. If we apply this distinction to the five comedies we have been examining, they are all folly plots except *The Taming of the Shrew,* and except for Oberon's enchantment of Titania in *A Midsummer Night's Dream;* Puck's action on the lovers is a folly plot. Now it may seem rather hard of me to classify as fools the noble young lords of *Love's Labour's Lost,* or Puck, or the people who made innocent and perfectly natural mistakes in *The Comedy of Errors;* so hard, in fact, that you may wonder whether the distinction itself is worth much. But I mean by it, as I said, only acting in error for whatever reason; and again, Petruchio is a wit in the sense that the main action is the working out of his comic stratagems to subdue Kate. The noble lords *do* act in error in undertaking an impossible project; Puck *does* make a mistake, although a perfectly natural one, and so do the people in *The Comedy of Errors.* If you remember the distinction I made, in Chapter I, between the ridiculous and the ludicrous —the ridiculous being that in which the mistake flows from some fault in the character of the agent, the ludicrous that in which it does not, but stems from ignorance of particular circumstances or from chance—we may say that the young lords are ridiculous, the others ludicrous.

But there are faults and faults. These are supposedly charming and brilliant young men of good character; their fault is a very slight one, simply the overzealousness of overearnest youth in setting its aim too high, no more than that. It springs from goodness; it is the kind of thing about which a friend might tease them; an enemy would have made it something far worse, or tried to make the characters ridiculous as a whole. And here we have, it seems to me, the clue to the comic quality of Shakespeare: his comic agents, if they are ridiculous, are only very slightly so—with one exception —and are viewed with affection; the others are ludicrous in their behavior, but are perfectly good people, and are also viewed with affection; they make mistakes which are perfectly excusable because perfectly natural, indeed practically unavoidable. Compare Shakespeare's handling of his characters with the way in which Ben Jonson handles his in *Volpone*, *The Alchemist*, and *The Silent Woman*. Jonson's agents have deep-seated and contemptible faults of character and disposition, and they are exposed as having them or expose themselves as having them. They are made *unlike* us to the point of caricature, sometimes being nothing more than an embodied vice; and their actions approach base action very nearly, almost to the point where the action itself becomes serious. Think of *Volpone*, for instance. As long as his actions threaten only rogues like himself, we do not take them seriously, for his victims are as guilty as himself; but had he been able to seduce the innocent Celia, we should have gone beyond the limits of the comic. Shakespeare has only a very small area of the unlike, and he treats this with affectionate humor.

The one exception I mentioned earlier is of course Falstaff in *The Merry Wives*. Falstaff is quite ridiculous and has plenty of vices; but these are presented as harmless to everyone except himself, and as causing him no great harm or pain except as they disable him for the execution of his projects; what we *chiefly* react to is the manifest silliness of his supposition that he can repair his fortunes by seducing the wives and the absurd consequences that this supposition brings about. But in the end no one really harms anyone; they will

> every one go home
> And laugh this sport o'er by a country fire;
> Sir John and all,

as Mistress Page says; and all feel about Falstaff as the dramatist himself seems to, with a mixture of affection and indulgence. Now if we seem to have been discussing character, let me point out that we have really been discussing the comic quality of plots; for you may remember that we defined plot as a morally determinate system of actions; as, that is, actions of a certain moral quality, so that character is implicated in it. Perhaps we can now move to the mechanical development of Shakespeare's plots—how he begins, complicates, and resolves his actions in his comedies.

Love's Labour's Lost has a main plot and an underplot which is pitched in a lower comic key. The essential incidents of the main plot are few: the young lords swear their vows of austere study; they encounter their ladies, fall in love and forswear their vows to make new ones to the ladies, each secretly sending his love a favor; all discover their fellows' secrets, three by being overheard, the fourth by the miscarriage of a love-letter, and they now decide to disguise themselves as Muscovites and call, in a party, to woo their ladies; the ladies are informed of their tiny intrigue, exchange their favors and don masks, so that each lover woos the wrong girl and all are sent packing; returning undisguised, they plead their love and each is told he must wait a year so that vows made "in heat of blood" and so often forsworn may be tested. The underplot is concerned with the suit of Don Adriano to the country wench Jacquenetta, and offers complication only in the miscarriage of the letter. Each plot moves in a series of short rushes to prolonged static situations. Each of these situations is simply used as an occasion for love-poetry and love-rhetoric (e.g., the strife between the lords as to which has the fairest lady, which ends in the forswearing of the vows to study in Act IV sc. iii), for some dubious wit and repartee, (much of which is very dull word-capping) both in the old doggerel metres and in prose, or for comic ornament of one sort or another. No doubt excellent comic capital might have been made out of the general idea; but every dramatic opportunity is frittered away in what is not so much the frivolity of the characters as the foolishness of the young author. Neither lords nor ladies are much distinguishable from one another; the little characterization they have is immediately and utterly ignored at the first opportunity for some dismal efforts of wit. All of them talk alike and think alike and act alike; and outside of occasional passages of eloquence, there is little here to hint at the greatness to come. We have here a young poet who wants to write a play and who does not know how. He wants complication, but does not know how to develop it; he can invent no better device than a miscarriage of letters; to effect his resolution, he must kill off the King of France, who is quite outside the plot. His idea of a dramatic speech is a lyric; if not that, a piece of rhetoric; if not that, a feeble sally of wit. And he is neither quite sure of what is going on, nor how he feels about it, nor how his characters do. For example, when the death of the King is announced, we are told that "the scene begins to cloud," but the Princess does not seem to think so; she and her ladies are readily convinced that they have time for more love-rhetoric, and time to hear out the rest of the show they have been watching.

The Comedy of Errors, closely as it follows in time, shows far greater skill of contrivance. To begin with, Shakespeare has learned how to find the proper magnitude of the action, and how to develop the action itself to that magnitude. The action of *Love's Labour's Lost* is much too short for the play; it is padded, as I said, with rhetoric, poetry, quibbling, divertissements, and unnecessary episodes (such as the deer-hunt) to the point where it is nearly shapeless; but the action of *The Comedy of Errors* is almost of the right magnitude. I suppose that this question of magnitude is one of the subtlest matters of dramatic art; at any rate, even very great dramatists seem to have trouble with it. I am speaking not of the *physical* length of the play but of the development of the action itself to just the right point of maximum effectiveness and plausibility so that there is not an incident too few or too many. We might illustrate this from *The Comedy of Errors.* Shakespeare is basing on Plautus' *Menaechmi,* and he also wants a five-act play, full-length by Elizabethan standards. But the Plautine action is—in terms of the number of episodes—much too short for this. What to do? There are various possibilities: he can pad, as he did in *Love's Labour's Lost,* at the cost of some of the comic energy; he can represent each incident on a much larger scale than Plautus (that will of course slow up the action); he can extend the string of errors (that will grow tedious after a time); and he can add more lines of action; or even add a by-plot (that will be bound to draw some attention from the main action). Each of these possibilities carries a disadvantage with it; so he solves his problem by doing all of them in moderation. You find him padding in such scenes as Act III sc. i, in more of that sickening doggerel repartee, and in the following scene, both in the love duet of Luciana and Antipholus of Syracuse and in the positively degraded geography of Dromio's kitchen wench; he expands nearly all the incidents of error; he extends the string by adding a second pair of twins, plus a few more people to be confused; he adds another line of action (the Luciana love-business) and the by-plot of Aegeon and Adriana—which by the way forces him to add later deus ex machina complications in order to effect the resolution. He is still adding extraneous matter, though to a lesser degree, and some of it works counter to his comic purpose. The Aegeon business, I think, is a great mistake; it is much too serious, and we either forget it until the resolution, in which case it might as well not be there, or we remember it, in which case it casts an unpleasant shadow over what should be pure fun. And by the way, he still tends to break character in order to allow rhetoric or lyric poetry or "wit"; the geography questions of Antipholus in the scene just mentioned are completely out of character. Indeed, in these two plays I doubt whether he has managed to create a character. And here is the thing, perhaps: I do not think Shakespeare is much of a joke-maker; his wit runs rather to character and action and situation. That is, a funny remark is funny in him, not in the abstract, but because some particular person has made it. Think of Bottom's "Methinks I have a great desire to a bottle of hay: good hay, sweet hay, hath no fellow." This is Shakespeare's proper vein. It does not take too long for him to find it.

For in *A Midsummer Night's Dream* he seems to solve all his problems at once. The plot is of magnificent architecture: it has three main plot-lines, the line of Bottom and his friends, that of the lovers, and that of Titania and Oberon. The last serves both to complicate and to resolve itself and the other two. All are not merely framed by the marriage preparations of Theseus and Hippolyta but intimately related to them, for Bottom & Co. are preparing entertainment for the wedding night, the day of the wedding is the one on which Hermia must decide whether to marry as her father wishes or suffer the penalty the Athenian law imposes, and Titania and Oberon, long separated, have come to bless the bridal bed of their favorites. The framing action and the three plot-lines are thematically as well as consequentially related, for all deal in one way or another with love: the royally dignified love of Theseus and Hippolyta, which sets off the comic loves of the others; the elfin love-strife of Titania and Oberon; the passions of the young Athenian lovers; even the line of Bottom & Co., for Bottom is briefly Titania's great love, and also the play the "rude mechanicals" are preparing is a travesty of unfortunate love.

I said a moment ago that the Titania-Oberon line served both to complicate and to resolve itself and the other two. Consider how this is worked out. The coming marriage brings together Titania and Oberon, who have been long at strife over a changeling child; Titania's persistent refusal to yield the child produces Oberon's trick in revenge; Titania gives up the child in order to be freed of the enchantment; and, the cause of quarrel removed, they are reconciled. The rude mechanicals plan to present their play; Puck, finding them rehearsing too close to "the cradle of the fairy queen," drives them away by his enchantment of Bottom; that enchantment and Titania's involvement in it threaten to make the performance of the play impossible; the lifting of the enchantments puts everything back on course. Hermia and Lysander, again, are fleeing Athens to escape the law and marry; the other pair pursue; the efforts of Oberon and Puck to resolve the love-problem first complicate it, then bring it to happy solution. In each case we have, then, an undertaking; then interference with it; finally, the happy conclusion of it. There is none of the incidental complication or resolution which mars the earlier plays; once the dramatic premises have been expounded, everything follows in consequence.

Shakespeare by now has fully mastered the massive multilinear plot which he is to use so often for such different purposes: many lines of action, contrasting with or mirroring one another, each enhancing the effect of the others, intricately entangled. In *A Midsummer Night's Dream*—complicated as the plot is—everything is perfectly clear. There are no unnecessary incidents; there is none of the plot-lines but would suffer if another incident were added to it—for example, another turnabout in the relations of the Athenian lovers would spoil the play. There are no unnecessary characters and there are no protatic characters—that is, those who are in the play only for the purpose of dramatic exposition. Fantastic as the range of character is, character is kept on all levels; the fairies neither think nor speak like the humans; Oberon is as different from Titania as Puck is from both. The Athenian lovers are all different: Helena is tall, gentle, timid; Hermia little, fiery, shrewish; Lysander is of more passionate, perhaps more violent nature than Demetrius— compare for example his rejection of Hermia with Demetrius's of Helena. And there is no extraneous matter of any kind in the play; we have none of those dismal passages of factitious wit, even from Bottom's crowd, no flights into rhetoric or poetry for their own sake. Marvelous as are the rhetoric and poetry in this play, they are ruled throughout by their dramatic purpose. Look at the little duets between Lysander and Hermia and Hermia and Helena in the first scene; they are a device carried over from the earlier plays, but how differently the device is used! Everything here is fitted to its function.

And, as to the specifically *comic* quality of the play, we have the absurd here in a thousand forms: Bottom's officious vanity and ignorance; the esteem his fellows have for him; his complacency in his enchantment, in his unwondering acceptance of the fairies, under Titania's tender ministrations; the Pyramus and Thisbe play (compare this little gem with the dull Nine Worthies business in *Love's Labour's Lost!*); the quarrels of Titania and Oberon, so fierce that

> all their elves for fear
> Creep into acorn cups and hide them there;

Titania's infatuation with him; the whole mixup of the Athenian lovers, the tall Helena's fear of the little Hermia; the tiny activities of the fairies—these are supposed to be tiny fairies—they make war on bats for their leathern wings to make coats of, they can creep into acorn cups, they can be overflowed by the broken honey-bag of a bumblebee, a cast snake's skin is "wide enough to wrap a fairy in"; all so many dainty absurdities of fancy; and so much else. Note, by the way, that Shakespeare has created his own fairy world; these are not like any who existed before or after; and note how admirably their general character fits the play; you could not substitute Walter de la Mare's malicious and disturbing fairies for them, nor Yeats', nor any other.

The Taming of the Shrew and *The Merry Wives of Windsor* are inferior both in mechanical construction and in comic force; I should not be surprised to learn that they were earlier plays, for they show some of Shakespeare's earlier faults. *The Taming of the Shrew* has a string-plot as its main action, a plot of incidents simply strung together: a mere series of tricks which Petruchio plays upon Kate, and they might have gone on endlessly, for there is no particular reason why she should reform at one point rather than another. And the tricks simply strike me as silly and lacking invention: what is the point of, and where is the fun in, Petruchio's outrageous costume for his wedding for instance? I have never seen this play without observing much forced heartiness on the part of the actors: a sign, I think, of their recognition of and embarrassment at its real deficiency in the comic. A number of incidents are so improbable and pointless that it is difficult to believe the dramatist knew what he was doing: for instance Kate's binding and beating her sister Bianca in the first scene of Act II, or the extremely artificial and unsatisfactory conclusion. The underplot, too, shows little invention.

The Merry Wives of Windsor also has a string-plot as its main action: nothing more than the three tricks which the wives play on Falstaff. The two escapes of Falstaff, one in the buck-basket, the other in woman's clothing, are stock tricks of farce and show little imagination; the last trick, in which Falstaff is decoyed into a wood and tormented by children pretending to be fairies, is neither funny nor convincing. Compare any of this with the Gadshill robbery business in *Henry IV;* at once it is clear that the comic invention of the one is as inferior to that of the other as the Falstaff of *The Merry Wives of Windsor* is to the Falstaff of Prince Hal. Indeed, Falstaff is not really suited to this plot. The great Falstaff is both wit and butt, and much of the comedy about him depends upon the fact that we are never quite sure which he will turn out to be; but in *The Merry Wives of Windsor,* he is butt simply. Half of him is missing; and to take that half away is to leave less than half. This play, too, I have never seen played without forced merriment and assumed gusto on the part of the actors.

The dramatic art of Molière is in sharp contrast to Shakespeare's. The Shakespearean comic plot is, we saw, characteristically massive, multilinear, even multiple-storied. Plots of this kind are likely to require frequent changes of scene and cover great stretches of time. Of the five comedies we examined, only *The Comedy of Errors* restricts its action to the events of a single day, and only *Love's Labour's Lost* keeps the unity of place; otherwise, they range well beyond the three unities. I do not mean that Molière always keeps the unities, for he does not—for example, he does not in *Don Juan;* my point is rather that whereas the Shakespearean action is sprawling and extensive, the Molièrean is characteristically much less extensive; and that this difference in the magnitude of the action brings about characteristic differences in the representation of it on the stage. What underlies this difference in the magnitude of action is the sharp difference between the English and the French conceptions of a scene as part of an act. The French scene is determined by the entrance or exit of a character; the English, by either a change of place or the unity of an incident; and the French early adopted the device of *liaison des scènes*, binding scene to scene so that the stage remains continuously occupied throughout an act. Molière does not always follow this practice—see *L'Etourdi*, for example; but it is his general, though not invariable, method. The chief consequence is that whereas with French dramatists the time required for performance might approximate or even equal the time span of the depicted action, English dramatists could permit the latter to far exceed the former. But other strictures follow on this. A French dramatist had to contrive his plot chiefly of essential incidents, eliminating as much as possible those which simply supplied the conditions for incidents. He had, further, to make these few and closely connected, so that consequence followed cause immediately or almost so; he had to begin as close as possible, therefore, to the complication, and to have the complication itself such that it could be resolved without requiring too many things to happen. Obviously, thus, the multilinear plot and the multiple story were almost interdict for him; if he wanted to introduce a subplot, he had to practice even stricter economy. What could not be conveyed by the action itself had to be left outside the plot, and if germane to the effect, had to be expounded by the narrative of one character to another, or by soliloquy or aside.

Thus *Hamlet* or *Macbeth* would have looked very different had a French poet written them. You would not have had shuttlings from platform to throne room to hall to platform, or heath to field to heath to castle. More importantly, the whole shape of the action would have been different. Had Shakespeare written *Tartuffe*, he could have begun with the first encounter of Orgon with Tartuffe; Molière had to treat their association as a long-established fact, and you are given the background of it in one of the most fantastically skillful expositions ever penned by a dramatist. By the way, such exposition itself had of course to fit naturally into the action, that is, to be established as a probable act.

But the differences go beyond differences of plot and scenario contrivance. As Shakespeare matures, he goes more and more into circumstantial detail, keeping the universal but making it seem individual, so that ultimately a whole host of living men and women seem to be set before us. Think of Falstaff, for instance: we know all about him—how he looked, how he walked, how he dressed, what he ate and drank and how much of each, all that pertains to his personality as well as his character; even minor personages are not scanted, though drawn in less detail. And Shakespeare handles settings in the same way; think how much you know about the wood in *A Midsummer Night's Dream*, or Macbeth's castle, or the palace at Elsinore.

Molière does none of this. He has his great characters, too, very sharply drawn; but they are given only such traits as are absolutely necessary to the play; and they are as close to the universal as possible. Everything you know about Harpagon relates to his incredible miserliness, everything you know about Tartuffe relates to his being an infamous scoundrel who is masquerading as a religious man. These figures are alive and true; but they are true as caricatures and not as portraits; they are alive as caricatures may be, but not as portraits may. In the same way, although the whole action commonly happens in one place, you never learn anything much about the place; it is just a square or someone's house or whatever else is most convenient for the action, and that is all.

And of course their diction is very different. Shakespeare's abounds in images and metaphors and similes and rhetorical ornament of all kinds; and, as I complained, much word-play. But this is Molière's view of word-play:

What a fine thing to introduce into conversations in the Louvre those old puns, picked up from the mud of the market and of Maubert Square. What a charming way for courtiers to talk! and how much wit a man displays when he says to you, Madame, you are in the place Royale, and everyone sees you from three leagues distance from Paris, because everyone regards you with favor [there is a pun here on *voir de bon oeil* and *Bonneuil*, a village outside Paris]; isn't that gallant and witty?[1]

He uses few metaphors save those which were in current use,

like "flame" for "love," as we say, "an old flame of mine."
The following passage is about as rhetorical as Molière ever
gets:

What! You make no distinction between hypocrisy and devo-
tion? You wish to speak of them in the same terms, and render
the same honor to a mask as to a face? Put artifice on the same
level as sincerity, confound appearance with truth, value the
ghost as much as the living man and false money as highly as
good?[2]

Shakespeare employs the whole range of styles, from high
to low, to make different characters speak differently as they
feel different emotions in different situations; Molière's
characters speak on much the same level, unless they happen
to speak some dialect, like Charlotte and Pierrot in *Le Festin
de Pierre*, or unless some affectation of speech is being ridiculed, as in *Les Précieuses Ridicules*. Nor is there much
distinction between the style of the verse and that of the
prose, except that exigencies of rhyme and metre sometimes force Molière to pad out a line, or to choose words
less apt than those he should have used had he not been so
fettered.

Working thus as he does with much stricter requirements
of plot, within a more stringent format of scenario, with
more restricted devices of characterization and language, it
is inevitable that Molière should have a much narrower
range of the comic than Shakespeare. Yet we must qualify
this: Molière was able to handle the wicked, the mean, the
base in comedy as Shakespeare apparently was not. La Harpe
touches on this point very nicely, I think, in commenting on
Tartuffe:

Suppose one proposed to a comic poet, a writer with a good
deal of talent, such a plan for a play as the following: A man
in the meanest circumstances manages, by his outward piety, to

impose upon a good man, well-intentioned and credulous, to the point where the latter takes the pious hypocrite into his own home, supplies his sustenance, offers him his daughter in marriage, and deeds his entire property to him. What recompense does he have?—the supposed devout begins by seeking to seduce the wife of his benefactor, and not succeeding, uses the deed of gift to expel the benefactor from his home, and employs papers with which his benefactor had entrusted him to bring about the arrest and imprisonment of the man who had heaped benefits upon him. I can hear the poet exclaim: How horrible! An audience would never endure the spectacle of such atrocities in the theatre, and a monster of that sort is inadmissible in comedy. But Molière comes forward and says: It is I who have imagined this subject that makes you tremble, and when you see how it is handled it will make you laugh, and it will be a comedy.[3]

How does Molière do it? La Harpe thinks that he does it through the fact that any mask which people wear—that is, any false pretense—necessarily entails the ridiculous. I am not sure of that in general; I am certain that is not what is operative here. It is not Tartuffe who is the comic protagonist and the figure primarily ridiculous; it is his dupe, Orgon, who in his infatuation with Tartuffe commits one extravagance after another. The ridicule is directed not so much at the hypocrite as at the man foolish enough to be taken in by the hypocrite, although nearly everyone else sees through the mask; who persists in his blind folly, ignoring his own interest and the interest of others, despite warnings; who would rather believe Tartuffe than his own wife and son, and who has to witness Tartuffe's baseness himself before he realizes the truth. In a word, it is not baseness which Molière makes comic, but folly. Tartuffe himself is ridiculous only when someone suddenly exposes the absurdity of one or another of his pretences, as in the following passage, in which he tries to impress Dorine, who sees through him, with his great modesty:

Dorine is wearing a fashionable low-cut gown.

TARTUFFE (taking a handkerchief from his pocket):

  O! for goodness sake (madame) I beg you,

Accept this handkerchief from me, before we talk.

DORINE: What do you mean?

TARTUFFE: Cover your breast, I dare not look at it;

  Souls are injured by such sights, they make for guilty thoughts.

DORINE: You must be very susceptible to temptation, then; flesh makes a great impression on your senses. . . . Myself, I am not so readily seduced; I could see you nude from head to foot, all your skin would not tempt me.[4]

Here Tartuffe is ridiculous, not because he is pretending, but because the pretence itself is unmasked as absurd by the very person he was seeking to impress.

Yet indeed Molière could make the base itself ridiculous by showing its consequences in absurd action. This is the device he uses in *The Miser,* and the use of it is typical in the following passage, in which the miser Harpagon is anxious to recover his stolen treasure. His servant Maitre Jacques has falsely accused Valère, another servant, of the theft. Observe this wonderful inquisition:

HARPAGON: And on what grounds do you believe this?

JACQUES: On what grounds?

HARPAGON: Yes.

JACQUES: I believe it . . . on the ground that I believe it.

HARPAGON: Have you seen him hanging around the place where I hid my money?

JACQUES: Yes, truly. Where was it, your money?

HARPAGON: In the garden.

JACQUES: Exactly the very place I saw him, in the garden. What did you keep your money in?

HARPAGON: In a strong-box.

JACQUES: There you are. I saw him with a strong-box.

HARPAGON: And this strong-box—what was it like?

JACQUES: What was it like?

HARPAGON: Yes.

JACQUES: It was like . . . it was like a strong-box.

CONSTABLE: Naturally. But describe it a bit.

JACQUES: It was a big strong-box.

HARPAGON: The one stolen from me was little.

JACQUES: Oh yes, it was little if you look at it that way; but I call it big because of what it contained.

CONSTABLE: What color was it?

JACQUES: What color?

CONSTABLE: Yes.

JACQUES: It was colored . . . well, a certain color . . . help me say it.

HARPAGON: Huh?

JACQUES: Wasn't it red?

HARPAGON: No, gray.

JACQUES: Well, yes, gray-red; that's what I meant.

HARPAGON: There's no doubt whatsoever; that's it, beyond doubt. Come, constable, write out the warrant.[5]

We have here, then, in Shakespeare and Molière, two great comic playwrights as different in spirit and invention as in technique. Molière is pure comedian; his talents lie wholly within the comic sphere; his wit ranges from pure fear to the most merciless ridicule. For Shakespeare, on the other hand, the comic, as we have defined it, is almost incidental to his genius: for what would have been enough to bring fame to any other man is only a small part of his achievement, and perhaps, except for *A Midsummer Night's Dream*, a lesser aspect of his talent. The sharp ridicule which is part of Molière's gift is impossible to him; his true wit is genial; he cannot ridicule the base; instead it evokes his anger, and he must treat it seriously.

Each of these authors, in his own way, subsumes the whole history of comedy; each in his way transforms it so greatly that all future writers must work in his shadow.

CHAPTER VI

Moderns

Consider the following story. A servant of a noble family, entrusted with the care of its infant heir, accidentally becomes separated from the child and in terror of the consequences flees. A rich old aristocrat finds the babe, adopts it, raises it to manhood, and on dying leaves the foundling the bulk of his estate. He also makes him guardian of a young girl, an orphan relative. The young man raises the girl in secrecy in the country to protect her from evil influence. The heir falls in love with a young noblewoman of a neighboring city, and she with him; her family, however, forbids the marriage on discovering that he is of unknown origin. The lovers determine to be faithful to each other nevertheless; and when the youth returns to his estate, his beloved follows him. During his sojourn in the city, the youth had let slip the secret of the existence as well as of the whereabouts of his ward to a young friend, a relative of his beloved; the friend seeks out the ward, falls in love with her, and wishes to marry her. A parent of the foundling's beloved, coming in pursuit of her, approves the friend's marriage to the ward; but the foundling-guardian refuses to permit this unless the parent permits his marriage as well. This request, however, is denied as before; and matters are at an impasse when the parent happens to recognize the ward's tutor as the servant who years ago had lost the child. The tutor reveals that a certain token had been left with the child; on hearing this, the foundling produces the token and identifies himself, thus, as the lost elder brother of his friend. This removes all obstacles to the marriages, and the happy lovers are left rejoicing.

Where has one heard a tale like that before? Separated families, adopted foundlings, love forbidden, resolution brought about through a recognition by tokens—the New Comedy, of course. Originally Euripidean; developed into comic matter in the New Comedy; picked up by Plautus and Terence, passed on to the Renaissance, showing up in many different forms, drama and fiction, tragedy, comedy, romance, whatnot; you may find it or an analogue of it in the *Clementine Recognitions*, in the comic epic of *Tom Jones*, Stevenson's *Kidnapped*, Joyce's *Stephen Daedalus*, William Gaddis' *The Recognitions*.

But since evidently this little tale or its analogues can assume so many different forms, undergo such miraculous shape-shiftings, now to one effect, now to its contrary, now producing pity and fear, now laughter, an important question arises: what determines it as one thing or another, producing this effect or that, all in such apparently endless variety? In Chapter I, I observed that we take seriously anything about which we have a complex opinion—that is, an opinion compounded of opinions that something is good or bad, in a considerable degree, more certain than not, more imminent than remote, involving persons in whose fortunes we have some interest (this includes not merely ourselves and friends but also our enemies of course). If this is correct, we can make our story extremely serious by telling the story so that it affords evidence that something is extremely good or bad, inevitable or almost so, imminently at hand, involving persons whose good or evil fortunes are of the greatest possible value to us. On the other hand, we can diminish seriousness by diminishing degree in any of these topics; we can turn it into the comic (the *contrary* of the serious) by rendering absurd any part of the complex opinion on which seriousness rests, and we can render it more comic as we increase the degree of absurdity or make more and more of the grounds for seriousness absurd.

Take the recognition scene in our story, for example. If we wish to handle it seriously, we must make the personages such that their fortunes are important to us, the recognition itself must be important to them, and the whole thing —including the devices which bring about recognition— must be made as credible as possible, for we also take things seriously according to the degree of belief we accord to their possibility or probability. (If you believe the Martians are invading us, you take this seriously; if you believe it impossible that they could, you will find ridiculous those who do take it seriously.) So, as to the devices which produce recognition, if you wanted seriousness these would have to be jewels or garments or scars or something that might plausibly identify someone; but if you made them some object with ludicrous associations, or else something that could not possibly identify anything, you would drop straight out of the serious into the comic. Again, if you want the lovers taken seriously, their passion must seem to have a believable cause; but if you do what Stephen Leacock did with his lovers in one of his stories—without their ever having met, she falls in love with him when she sees his underwear hanging on the line, he with her when he sees her name painted on a fence—why, that is another matter again.

And so, to come back to our tale: if you make the instrument of recognition an ordinary handbag into which an absent-minded nurse stuffed the baby, meanwhile wheeling off the manuscript of her voluminous love-novel in the perambulator, and if both girls fall in love with their lovers before they meet them, simply because they are both supposedly named Ernest, you will drop straight into comedy. And now the secret must be out, if you have not already guessed it: we have been talking about *The Importance of Being Earnest.*

This comic tinkering with an old tale is by no means the only thing that Oscar Wilde does to produce his comedy; but it is the thing which is most important for the purposes of this chapter, and I shall want to return to it presently. For the moment let us look at what else he does. He does quite a number of things. He devaluates the action by making all the characters rather silly and trivial persons. As he must if he is to have girls falling in love with men because of their names, he contrives equally silly lovers for them, who invent imaginary persons to afford pretexts for getting off on their little sprees, and who manage to get quite as excited about cucumber sandwiches, muffins, and cigarette-cases as about their loves. But chiefly it is his dialogue, as you know, which produces the comic effect; not by the famous Wildean epigrams (there are, as a matter of fact, few epigrams in this play), nor even by the passages of pure nonsense such as Algy's divagations, which are flatly called "nonsense" by John. Rather it is a device which is as old as comedy, and which yet was perhaps never before employed so systematically: the remark with its immediate comic reversal whether coming from the speaker or someone else. Remove these comic reversals and you get perfectly reasonable dialogue, steadily advancing the progress of the scene; put them back, and everything is different. Take for example the scene in Act I in which Lady Bracknell is questioning Jack in order

to determine whether he is worthy of Gwendolen. First let
us take out the comic reversals:

LADY BRACKNELL: Do you smoke?
JACK: Yes.
LADY BRACKNELL: How old are you?
JACK: Twenty-nine.
LADY BRACKNELL: What is your income?
JACK: Between seven and eight thousand a year.
LADY BRACKNELL: In land or investments?
JACK: In investments, chiefly . . . I have a country house with
   some land of course, attached to it.
LADY BRACKNELL: You have a town house, I hope?
JACK: Well, I own a house in Belgrave Square.
LADY BRACKNELL: What are your politics?
JACK: Well, I am afraid I really have none.
LADY BRACKNELL: Are your parents living?
JACK: I have lost both my parents.

Now let us put them back in:

LADY BRACKNELL: . . . Do you smoke?
JACK: Well, yes, I must admit I smoke.
LADY BRACKNELL: I am glad to hear it. A man should always have
   an occupation of some kind. There are far too many idle men
   in London as it is. How old are you?
JACK: Twenty-nine.
LADY BRACKNELL: A very good age to be married at. I have always
   been of opinion that a man who desires to get married should
   know either everything or nothing. Which do you know?
JACK: I know nothing. . . .
LADY BRACKNELL: I am pleased to hear it. I do not approve of
   anything that tampers with natural ignorance. . . . What is
   your income?
JACK: Between seven and eight thousand a year.
LADY BRACKNELL: In land or investments?
JACK: In investments, chiefly.
LADY BRACKNELL: That is satisfactory. What between the duties
   expected of one during one's lifetime, and the duties exacted

from one after one's death, land has ceased to be either a profit or a pleasure. It gives one position, and prevents one from keeping it up. That's all that can be said about land.

And so on, to

LADY BRACKNELL: . . . Now to minor matters. Are your parents living?
JACK: I have lost both my parents.
LADY BRACKNELL: To lose one parent, Mr. Worthing, may be regarded as a misfortune; to lose both looks like carelessness.

Here we have, I think, a matter of dialogue *as such*. It is not plot: not one of these reversals is required by the plot, and some indeed are inconsistent with it. Jack's parentage is not, in Lady Bracknell's phrase, a minor matter; in fact it is the matter on which the whole plot hinges. Nor is character involved here; these remarks do not flow from Lady Bracknell's character or serve to characterize her in any way; on the contrary, they are rather inconsistent with her character —for example, *she* does not think parentage a "minor matter." The playwright is simply intervening at every possible point to upset what his characters are saying; but these comic reversals do not lead us to any consistent view on his part or on the part of his characters; they merely reverse anything that the audience has been anticipating; they are purely incidental and they are indeed mechanical, for once you have the formula you can produce such wit indefinitely. It is delightful; but it is also mechanical. It is also perfectly empty. This is not really supposed to be a picture of London society. Wilde is merely teasing, to no point except your amusement, with no particular ideas in his head. *The Importance of Being Earnest* is the only play of Wilde's that is comedy in our sense, but in fact it involves no great amount of comic art; it is not comedy so much as theatrical *badinage*.

No one, to my knowledge, has ever accused Bernard Shaw of lacking ideas, although many people have thought that his ideas were upside down; indeed, one writer remarks that Shaw stands on his head and then blames the world for taking a view opposite to his. Yet in certain respects he resembles Wilde. Wilde, we saw, "tinkered with form"; he took one of the crucial scenes of comedy—the recognition scene, on the probability of which the resolution ordinarily depends even in comedy—and turned it into sheer absurdity. This is a small if significant thing in Wilde; his comedy does not depend on it much; but for Shaw it is one of the chief parts of his dramatic method. He loves to take a story, or a piece of history, or a dramatic or fictional form or convention, and tinker with it. Now, a story or piece of history or literary forms or conventions always represent established beliefs, settled opinions, as the slightest reflection will assure you; these are what you must suppose if you are to accept the tale or whatever. *Cinderella* supposes among other things that you think marriage with a prince is very desirable. You have certain opinions about historical figures: what do you think of Nero or Richard III? What of Socrates or Joan of Arc? You have settled opinions about literary forms—otherwise my saying something was melodrama or tragedy would mean nothing to you. And about literary conventions; for example, the convention that the narrator in a murder mystery is never the murderer—do you remember how *The Murder of Roger Ackroyd* fooled everybody by upsetting this convention?

So we have embodiments of opinion here, so to speak, and the more ancient and widespread the tale or the history, the more representative it is, generally speaking, of settled opinion. Now opinion has two effects we must observe: first, it is the most important cause of emotion. If you think a rattlesnake is about to strike you, you will feel fear even if your opinion is false; if you do not think so, you will not be frightened even if one is actually about to strike. Second, opinion is related to anticipation; if you believe soldiers are boastful, you will expect a soldier to boast; and if your expectation is falsified, you will be surprised in proportion to the strength of your conviction and to the extent to which the fact turns out to be opposite to it.

Shaw knew all this very well, and based his method on it, taking out the crucial probabilities involved in fiction or history, and replacing them with their opposites. Is a marriage a happy ending? Look at *Widowers' Houses*. Does a soldier carry guns into battle? Look at *Arms and the Man*. Was Cleopatra a siren, are men who denounce God irreligious, are arms manufacturers ruthless and inhuman monsters, did the Christian martyrs suffer because of their great faith? Look at *Caesar and Cleopatra, The Devil's Disciple, Major Barbara, Androcles and the Lion.* Is burning at the stake an agonizing and unforgettable experience? Read *Saint Joan.*

Yet this is not, as in Wilde, a mere conversion into opposites, without significance. Wilde's witticisms fall into two kinds; those which depend simply upon reversal of what is said, and those which, through reversal of *what is said,* also effect the reversal of the speech as action. For instance, "I can resist everything except temptation" is merely a self-reversing statement; "I hear her hair is turned quite gold with grief" turns an apparently sympathetic remark into the opposite, and so reverses the speech *as action.* But Wilde is merely playful, whereas Shaw is serious about his opposites; they may not be wholly true for him, but they are truer than the beliefs they replace. So there are two sides to his technique: the destructive dialectic and the constructive. Shaw can be witty in both, but the former produces most of the comic effect.

In effect he is saying, in many different ways, "That is not what happened at all," "He or she wasn't anything like that," "He did that for a quite different reason," and things of the sort. What he *converts* into opposites is either action or character; for example, Dick Dudgeon faces the gallows not motivated by love of Judith, as both she and the audience have been led to suppose (for love was the stock theatrical motive in such cases, as Shaw himself observes), but for himself, in obedience to the law of his own nature; that is the Shavian conversion of an act; and. Caesar and Cleopatra and Napoleon and Don Juan and Joan of Arc and others are all very different from the conventionally accepted images of them; that is the conversion of character. This device has its hazards, for conversion into contraries will not always yield an existent thing. For example, as Francis Bacon observed, the existence of poisons which kill does not imply the existence of medicines which restore the dead to life. Similarly, the contrary of a given act which is implausible is not necessarily itself plausible, and Shaw's dialectic sometimes leads him to the invention of implausible characters and implausible acts. I am not thinking of the improbabilities in his farcical scenes, for they do not matter there; I am thinking of Marchbanks and Burgess in *Candida* and Bentley in *Misalliance* and the whole riff-raff in his play *Geneva*. The first act of *The Devil's Disciple* is full of improbabilities: would a man of Dick's character have been a smuggler? Would he have behaved as he did toward the minister and his wife, especially on an occasion like that? The last act of *Heartbreak House*, too, is full of improbabilities.

Shaw professed to have great contempt for plots, particularly the well-made plots: "I avoid plots," he says, "like the plague. . . . My procedure is to imagine characters and let them rip." In fact, however, as Eric Bentley and others have observed, he contrives plots and contrives them with care; and this remark is not merely misleading but fallacious; for the question is not one of the way in which you do things but of what you end up with; and these characters allowed to "rip" have a curious way of confining their rippings to what the plot demands. This is the kind of thing that will happen by chance when those famous imaginary monkeys manage to type out the works of Shakespeare. Critics have often cited the passage in *The Quintessence of Ibsenism* in which Shaw remarks that whereas the older form of play consisted of exposition, complication, and resolution, the newer consists of exposition, complication, and discussion, with the discussion coming in at any point in the play; and we are supposed to think on this basis that something has replaced plot. But consider: *is* discussion a new element in comedy? What did Shaw think the Aristophanic agon was? Besides, this exposition-complication-resolution business is a confusion (transmitted from the fourth-century critic Donatus to later European criticism) between plot and scenario or dramatic format; between, as Aristotle would have put it, the parts of the chief qualitative part, which is plot, and the quantitative parts. Complication and resolution are parts of the complex plot; exposition is part of the scenario or format. But we need not be overtechnical about this. What Shaw has in mind is Ibsen's *A Doll's House,* and the fashion in which it ends: apparently all the problems have been solved, Nora goes into the bedroom, the audience anticipates the curtain at any moment, and then Nora reappears in street dress, and there is what Shaw calls a discussion. Certainly there is discussion here; but the discussion is part of the plot, indeed, of the resolution. All that really happens here is that the audience, on the basis of a theatrical convention, supposes that one consequence has followed; whereas now Ibsen will disclose the true probability-system of the plot, to produce the opposite consequence, which must be established as probable, and hence requires discussion which will lay bare the true issues involved in the action. It is inherently much more probable than the theatrical convention of ending in domestic bliss; but it never enters the heads of the audience, unless they are familiar with the play, and hence they are stunned by it. It is not the ending of a conventional well-made play; but it most certainly is the ending of the plot.

And perhaps all that is involved here is this: that when Shaw voices his contempt for plot, he means only the well-made plot. But plot and well-made plot are not quite the same thing. The so-called well-made plot, which is actually an ill-made plot, is simply a consequential chain of incidents; plot proper is a system of actions, deeds. The whole probability of the former depends upon the probability that one event as cause will produce another as effect. The probability of the latter includes not merely this, but the probability of character; that is, the probability that the agent, as a person of given character, will or will not do a given thing. You have met the well-made plot before, in the *Poetics* of Aristotle: it is simply a form of the characterless play, the kind, as Aristotle puts it, that may exist without character. The personages in a well-made play are puppets because they have no chance to choose, because the logic of events rules all, because their characters have been reduced to mere circumstances of the incidents; human agency has been reduced to natural force, and action has been reduced to event.

As Shaw remarks, to make such a reduction is to take all the significance out of human action: to put the sacrifice of

Christ or the burning of a Joan of Arc on the same level as the eruption of a volcano or the fall of a pebble. There is a great deal of difference between a powder keg's exploding on being ignited, and a man's igniting a powder-keg; the keg has neither sense nor mind and cannot choose; the man has sense and mind and can choose. There are no issues in the first except natural ones; the second involves distinctively human issues as well.

Now all Shaw's "discussion" amounts to, then, is this: discussion of the distinctively human issues in human action (though he is willing to discuss the natural element as well, even the possibility of altering human nature—see *Back to Methuselah*); the factors, in other words, which must be taken into account in deliberation; the dianoetic element in *proairesis* or choice. Someone acting out of passion or desire is being activated by natural forces alone, in Shaw's view, like the automata in the conclusion of the play just mentioned, and he has nothing but contempt for that—a contempt which explains his contempt for Shakespeare's *Antony and Cleopatra*. Nor is there any significance in someone's doing a villainous act because he is of a villainous nature, as he tells us in the Preface to *Saint Joan;* which is why he excludes villains from the play. The proper origin of human action is in will, the will as operating upon ideas and beliefs. And it is upon ideas and beliefs primarily that Shaw centers his attention: the process by which ideas and beliefs become actualized in, and determine the nature of, action. Thus the problem for him in *Saint Joan*, as his Preface declares, is not why villains should act villainously but through what causes good men might be brought to do an evil thing.

This is also, however, a reduction; for if we regard human beings simply as activated by their ideas, they become automata or puppets once more, only this time the puppets of their ideas rather than of their desires and passions. For man acts neither simply from passion nor from reason, but from these among other causes, including natural ones. And the Shavian reduction leads time and again to action as seen in one dimension only, or to character as depicted wholly in terms of ideas. Thus, at its worst, the Shavian discussion can become mere debate, as in Part II of *Back to Methuselah*, *The Gospel of the Brothers Barnabas*, where dramatic interest has to be sustained wholly by the opposition of ideas, and the Shavian character can at its worst become only someone who happens to hold a particular belief, and who has no emotions except those which are consequences of that belief. Moreover, in consequence the dramatic opposition between the persons of the play is often drawn not in terms of their differences as persons but in terms of the differences of their ideas; and this dialectical balance often leads to a dramatic imbalance, as in the play *Geneva*. But worse still: as we saw earlier, if you operate by taking a contrary view to the accepted one, time after time, there is no guarantee whatsoever that you will come out with a general position which is true, or for that matter, consistent. Suppose people generally believed that all men are rich; this is of course false; but if you assert the contrary, no men are rich, you will not be right either. Shaw's plays abound in such things: think of *Arms and the Man;* Raina believes that a man who leads a cavalry charge is the bravest of the brave; Bluntschli tells her that he is the man whose horse is running away with him. These are contrary views; but is the latter any more tenable than the former? The matter of inconsistency carries us much deeper; it can affect, for example, the entire framework of the plot, and in certain plays that is precisely what it does.

It does so for instance very notably in Shaw's most extended attack on the medical profession, *The Doctor's Dilemma*. The chief point of this play, as Shaw tells us, is that since men cannot be fair judges in cases where they themselves have an interest in a particular decision, doctors cannot either: the distinguished doctor Sir Colenso Ridgeon kills the husband of the woman he loves—a gifted but immoral man—by putting him into the hands of an incompetent physician, rather than treating him himself. From this we are supposed to infer that there is something wrong with the medical profession. But patently this has nothing to do with the medical profession. Insofar as a doctor acts *as a doctor*, he has no aim but the physical benefit of the patient; it will be indifferent to him as doctor whether he is treating a murderer about to be hanged or a saint on whom the world's welfare depends. If he assesses the moral character of the patient and kills or spares him accordingly, he is not acting as doctor but as judge; and in that case his action is not in accordance with his profession, but in violation of the very ethics and purpose of it. If he uses his medical skill to kill a rival, he is simply an assassin; and that is no part of the medical profession either. But here Shaw in his confusion would eat his cake and have it too: Ridgeon is corrupt because he abuses the powers of his profession and the profession is corrupt because of Ridgeon. There is another confusion: Shaw devotes much of the first act, and indeed much of the play, to suggest that medicine is all quackery and superstition; yet in that case the whole plot falls apart: Ridgeon could then no more kill than cure.

This is enough to suggest that if we are discussing the playwright as thinker, I do not think much of Shaw as thinker. As a thinker, he is less a philosopher than a crank; his ideas are neither original nor profound. Despite his great reputa-

tion for argument, he is really very poor at it; he is brilliant
and ingenious, but he is not sound; leaving aside his wonderful humanitarian instincts, he is only right by chance: that
is, he is right only when what he is attacking happens to be
wrong, and by no means always even then. But he *is* a great
playwright; and as long as the playwright has the upper hand
of the philosopher and propagandist, his contentiousness
makes for freshness, and his extravagance for fun.

His plays are as a rule longer than most; but his plots are
extremely brief, consisting of very few essential incidents.
Think of a few of them. *Widowers' Houses:* a young man
wishing to marry a wealthy girl discovers her money comes
from dishonorable sources; he proposes they live on his limited but adequate income and she refuses; he then discovers
his own income comes from the same sources, and forgets his
high principles to marry her. *Candida:* a husband permits
himself to be convinced that his wife loves another man; the
matter develops until it comes to her attention; she resolves
it. *Caesar and Cleopatra:* Caesar sets Cleopatra on the throne,
hoping she will become a model queen; instead she becomes
increasingly vicious; he abandons her. How does Shaw manage to make such short plots into full-length plays? He includes many episodes of high interest in themselves but not
necessary for the plot, as in *Caesar and Cleopatra;* he introduces apparent complications which are not really such (for
example, the whole business in *Arms and the Man* of the coat
and the photograph as threatening to betray Raina's harbor-
ing of Bluntschli—it threatens and threatens and comes to
nothing in the end), much incidental complication which
resolves itself and permits the plot to continue (like Doo-
little's visit to Higgins to take away Liza in *Pygmalion*),
lengthy but highly exciting expositions, as in *The Devil's
Disciple,* where the whole first act and part of the second is

exposition cunningly concealed. And, of course, by much discussion.

His favorite overall device is something that I will call *suspense of form*. It is a distinctively modern device, heavily relied upon by the more experimental playwrights, the avant-gardists, at any rate; and it consists in keeping the audience uncertain as to *what kind of play* they are witnessing: is it comic or serious, farce or tragedy, realism or fantasy? Thus—to give just a few examples from Shaw—*Arms and the Man* deliberately excites in you all the anticipations of the Graustarkian or *The Prisoner of Zenda* sort of romance; deflates this systematically; then winds up as a romance after all, though of another sort. *The Devil's Disciple* and *Captain Brassbound's Conversion* arouse all the anticipations of swashbuckling melodrama—the former, indeed, was written as a vehicle for the famous William Terris, who specialized in such plays—only to turn out to be something quite different. *Candida* pretends until well into the third act to be a triangle play—pretends so well that some critics, like Eric Bentley, still seem to take it as such, and discuss whether Candida is or is not a "black-widow spider" and whether a respectable wife would have put herself in a position where she would have to choose between her husband and another man; whereas Shaw's point is clearly that there is no choice, except in the overheated imaginations of the two men; Candida is unaware of what has been going on till the very last, when she determines to teach her husband a lesson; the general situation is in fact that of Molière's *The Imaginary Cuckold*. *Caesar and Cleopatra* evokes both erotic and heroic associations only to turn them into something else. *Pygmalion* suggests a love-romance so continuously that many—critics, audiences, even actors and directors—have refused to accept the Shavian ending as the true one. *Saint Joan* begins with farce, steadily deepens in seriousness until the Epilogue, there effects a comic reversal —not that of ordinary comedy, but of such as Shaw tells us the gods laugh at—only to end on the poignant note of Joan's final wondering cry. Meanwhile we have seen the saintliness and the miracles of the legendary Joan brushed aside, to be replaced by the miracles of the Shavian saint.

The use of suspense of form implies a systematic attack upon all the conventional—that is, habitual—emotional and moral responses of the audience, a breaking-up of established emotional and moral associations to replace them with new ones. It represents potentially—that is, according to the extent to which the dramatist employs it—the most complete assault that can be made upon an audience, since it subverts the whole emotional and moral context in terms of which people react to a play. It does not simply offer them a new idea or doctrine; it does not merely force the audience to view a given object in a new light, or respond to it with a different emotion; it undermines the very foundation of their emotions and moral judgments. It is of course bound to produce shock and bewilderment, for it demands of the audience not only the complete rejection of their presuppositions but also the maximal readjustment to newly established relations; and it runs the risk that the audience will hold on to the old and simply be puzzled by the new. We need not be surprised, therefore, to find that the more conventional critics of Shaw, as he himself tells us, accused him of representing villains as heroes and heroes as villains, or denied that he was writing plays at all. Even the late St. John Irvine once remarked that Shaw should never have written the Epilogue to *Saint Joan;* that without it you would have had a perfect tragedy. (He later altered this view somewhat in his book on Shaw.) I should say myself that if you left out the Epilogue you would have merely an unfinished and therefore unsatisfying play, of Lord knows what form, for the Epilogue contains the comic reversal.

What had been merely standard tinkering with form in Wilde's play becomes in Shaw, then, a subversion of specific form; but the avant-gardist playwrights—particularly the so-called "Absurdists"—carry Shavian technique, particularly the suspense of form, to even further extremes. I am by no means certain that the name "Absurdist" is a good one for these playwrights, and I am quite positive that dramatists of great heterogeneity in craft and purpose have been lumped together under this name. It would be pedantic to quarrel about this, however, and no doubt I have already been pedantic enough. I am interested here simply in what they do and what they effect by what they do; and they are relevant to this inquiry not because they write comedy (though some of them do) but because all of them, to one end or another, employ comic devices.

"All of them," I say naïvely; and yet it is a matter of some doubt who "they" are. Is Genet an Absurdist? Ghelderode? Pinter? Albee? Dürrenmatt? Some critics, to my wonder, have wished to include Wilder and O'Neill; some even Chekhov and Strindberg. Let us simply consider two of them briefly: Beckett and Ionesco.

In *Waiting for Godot* Beckett sets before us two tramps, who are waiting. Waiting for Godot. And who or what is Godot? The playwright leads us to frame one conjecture after another: God or man, hostile or friendly, hoped-for or feared; each cancels out in turn. The characters are simply waiting, for whomever; and if this represents life, the play seems to mean that life is no more than a waiting for something or someone that never appears. Meanwhile history goes on; tyrant oppresses slave, then their roles are reversed, as in Yeats' poem *The Great Day,* in which he represents history as one revolution following another. In one, "a beggar on horseback" lashes a beggar on foot; then the beggars change places, but "the lash goes on." So here, it would seem. But the two principal characters, while they are involved in that history, neither greatly affect it nor are greatly affected by it; they go on with their waiting for a Godot who does not come. I should call this play not so much an Absurdist as an Abstractionist play. The technique is one of negation; you will find it operating in the plays as well as the poems of Eliot, among others. Is it A you mean? No. B, then? No. Then C? No, etc., and when all the specifics are nullified, you move to a higher level of generality, where you begin all over again if you like, until you achieve the abstract. It is the opposite of the technique you use in the game called Twenty Questions; there in questioning you start with the general and work to the specific; here you move from specific to general.

In *Jack or the Submission* Ionesco uses a different technique. It is the very old technique of parody—but with what a difference it is used here! Ordinary parody simply converts what it mocks into the absurd; Ionesco converts it into the repulsive absurd. Here he takes a stock plot-pattern of the sentimental play and turns every element of the serious in it into absurdity, and wherever possible, the repellent. A fine if overidealistic young man falls out with his family because he refuses to conform to an old family tradition; the breach widens when he refuses to marry in accordance with the family's wishes; happily, he falls in love with the girl's even more beautiful sister, all are reconciled, the family rejoices. How many plays have been written along that general outline! But in Ionesco's play the tradition is liking potatoes cooked in grease; Jack refuses the girl who has two noses because she is not ugly enough; the girl he chooses has three noses (in fact, she tells us, three of everything); she seduces him on-stage (symbolically only, of course) by a tale of a burning horse galloping in the desert; the family shows its joy at the coming marriage by crawling obscenely about the stage on all fours; and, the stage directions tell us, the audience must be made to feel a deep sense of shame. This systematic devaluation of all that a plot may contain of conventional human values is typical of the better-known plays of Ionesco except *Rhinoceros;* you will find it in *The Bald Soprano* and *The Lesson,* and it is nearly run into the ground in *The Chairs.* Beckett's dialogue frequently moves in the Wildean fashion I have described to you; Ionesco's often turns into sheer gibberish. Beckett's stage action sometimes approaches a catatonic calm, as in *End Game;* Ionesco's, behavior in the violent ward of an asylum, with the actors ranting and screaming at each other.

These plays pretend to depict the world and the human condition. The world is absurd, the human condition is absurd, they must be said—not imitated or represented as, but *said*—to be absurd, and said by one device or another (symbol, allegory, dramatic metaphor) of implication. At the same time, the saying is not to take the form of a rational statement; and since dramatic form, like any form, reflects human values, it too must be negated: these plays are often subtitled "non-art," " anti-dramas," "non-plays." At their most extreme they seem to assault the principles as well as the conventions of drama; for these, too, reflect human values.

We have, in the Theatre of the Absurd, every device of comedy, indeed farce; but the effect is not supposed to be comic; the effect is supposed, like Ionesco's "deep shame," to be a serious one. Audiences do in fact laugh, sometimes uproariously; but they are not intended to, for this is supposedly not the comic but the serious absurd. Absurdist drama is in effect an off-shoot of the mock-heroic; the mock-heroic ridicules by comparisons with the heroic, that is, with a system of supreme values; the Absurdists attack the system of values itself.

And, speaking of values, what is the value of these plays? Or of all the plays discussed? Or further, how do we assess the value of any literary compositions? For the Absurdists, of course, that is an Absurd question and deserves an Absurd answer. But I am not an Absurdist, and I will try to answer it seriously. I think we can distinguish three levels of literary criticism:

The first is that practised by any reader or theatre-goer; it involves nothing more than taking in the work and judging it as pleasing or displeasing. The second is that practised by most literary critics in their technical analysis; it involves ascertaining how the effect of a work is produced through certain technical causes. It can tell us about the craftsmanship of the work as good or bad; but it may quite possibly tell us that the craftsmanship of *Treasure Island* is, as pure craftsmanship, equal to or better than that of *Moby Dick*. The third kind of criticism is not technical; perhaps it is not even literary. It involves an assessment of the effect as effect, or, in other words, of the experience we have in responding to the work precisely according to its value as an experience. This last kind of criticism must involve extra-literary, indeed extra-artistic considerations; for it must depend upon such values as we hold in life itself. We must invoke such values when we pronounce *Moby Dick* a greater book than *Treasure Island;* and we must practise such criticism because it is necessary to distinguish a *Moby Dick* from a *Treasure Island,* and because technical analysis cannot do this. To practise the second kind of criticism one need merely be a critic, and he can be taught to be this; to practise the third kind with any success one must be a human being of a somewhat high order. Whether one can be taught to be such a being is a matter of some dispute.

I wrote these words a number of years ago. I quote them because I wish to reaffirm them. If they are true words, art can never have a greater value than life, for it is ultimately measured by the values of life. The values, then, are prior; and anyone who laughs, anyone who is moved in any way by the comic, proclaims them. So long as there is the absurd, therefore, there cannot really be the Absurd; and so long as comedy and the comic are possible, so long will life and its values have meaning.

APPENDIX

The Analysis of Drama*

We hear a great deal nowadays of the necessity of approaching the play as a play, much as we still hear of the necessity of approaching the poem as poem. Almost every textbook, almost every anthology of drama, almost every history of drama insists that it is setting before us the play *as play;* and in nearly every instance this is done by expounding *the* concept of dramatic structure, *the* principles of dramatic form, and matters of the sort. The embarrassments which often follow attempts to utilize such statements are well known to teachers and students. In the first place, all such recitations suggest that the drama is a peculiarly static art, a suggestion which we seem to accept despite very obvious evidence that the drama has evolved, is evolving, and perhaps will continue to evolve in a pattern not too different from the pattern of evolution in any of the other arts. In the second place—and this is much more important—each time that we set up the fences which are to discriminate drama from non-drama, according to the recommended specifications, we find to our consternation that a great many of the works which we have regarded as the great monuments of human genius are miserably excluded, while a great many pieces of evident trash

* A paper presented before the National Council of Teachers of English in Boston, Massachusetts, on November 26, 1965.

rest securely within the pale. Charles Lamb tells us that *King Lear* and T. S. Eliot tells us that *Hamlet* are great works of art but poor plays; *The Green Goddess*, on the other hand, is a good play but completely worthless as art. You may be content with this state of affairs, either because you feel that drama has nothing to do with art or because you think that theory does not matter anyway; but if you are discontent with it, as I happen to be, you are faced with the problem of making theory commensurate with art; and the soundest way to treat this problem is to go back to the beginning and examine first principles.

How can we talk about the play *as play?* Let us observe at the outset that we cannot speak essentially (that is, of the *essence*) of anything simply by designating a particular example of it. We cannot for instance say, "Here is *Hamlet*, which is a play; now if we talk about *it*, we shall be talking about drama and what makes for drama." For *Hamlet*, or any other example, is many things other than a play, and we may quite legitimately discuss any of these. Nor shall we escape this difficulty by discussing what we tend to call the *structure* of *Hamlet*. A great many different structures can be found in *Hamlet*. *Hamlet* is a structure of letters, of syllables, of words; if we discuss it in terms of these, we shall be discussing its grammatical or its prosodic structure; a structure of antecedents and consequences—discussion of these will be discussion of its logical structure; a structure of devices for producing conviction—discussion of these will be discussion of its rhetorical structure. Also, as certain critics assure us, it has a structure of metaphors, of symbols, of images, of ideas, paradoxes, ironies, ambiguities, and so on. Each of these structures exists, we may assume, and each constitutes a whole of some kind, made up of parts which function within it. But it is self-evident that we shall have a number of quite different wholes, with quite different parts which function quite differently; and that consequently the analysis of each whole will prove to be a quite different analysis. This simultaneity of structures in a single object is by no means a phenomenon peculiar to art. A plant or an animal can also be considered—precisely because it *is*—such a multiplicity. A cell, a vein, a hair, a tooth, a hand, an arm, an eye is a whole; the nervous system is a whole, the skeleton is a whole, the circulatory system is a whole, the man is a whole; and all of these wholes have different parts which function differently. For whole and part are relative terms; as we stipulate different wholes, we shall have quite different parts, and our analyses will, as I said, differ for each.

It seems, thus, that if we discussed *Hamlet* from every conceivable aspect, much of our discussion would be relevant only slightly, if at all, to *Hamlet* as a play. We can separate the relevant from the irrelevant only by fixing on what we mean when we say that something is a play. You remember that in Dryden's *Essay of Dramatic Poesy* one of the speakers remarks that no one in the history of criticism had ever sought to define a play, to say precisely *what* a play is, and the following definition is presently offered: a play is "a just and lively image of human nature, representing its passions and humours, and the changes of fortune to which it is subject, for the delight and instruction of mankind." Now this is a very faulty definition—for example, it says nothing of the theatre or of acting, and so would apply also to the novel, the short story, or even lyric poetry; indeed, since it says nothing of the artistic medium, it would apply also to non-literary arts such as painting, sculpture, and music.

But its basic error goes much deeper than that; for the definition supposes that drama is a given *somewhat*, something of a given unitary nature, to be given one definition.

Drama is not a some*what*, but a certain *how*. When we use the term "drama" we do not designate any particular *form* of composition, but the manner or method of imitation used in a given form. The term "dramatic" has its parallel not in terms like "statue" or "poem," but in terms like "hand-hewn," "machine-stamped," etc. It signifies not a particular representation, but a *device or method used* in representation. (We do this with certain other artistic expressions, such as *sculpture, etching, collage, intaglio*—these all signify works through *methods*—just as works may also be called after the materials employed, as in *charcoal-sketch, water-color, oil-painting.*)

Certainly the method or manner of representation must enter into the definition of a specific form, such as tragedy—you will remember that it enters into Aristotle's definition, for example; but we must not confuse it with form itself. And such confusion is not only the root error of Dryden's effort, but of the greater part of dramatic theory. It is a very serious error, with very serious consequences. If we commit it, we shall have given a particular *means* the status of an *end;* we shall then be likely to think of it as something autonomous, with a function of its own; we are then likely to assign it laws and rules of its own, all drawn from its supposed "nature"; and we shall see the history of drama not in terms of evolving uses of certain devices, in evolving forms, but as something relatively static, and our dramatic theories will amount to what a contemporary dramatist has called "the short and dismal science of the theatre." Incidentally, also, we shall have produced the situation I spoke of earlier, in which the *King Lears* and *Hamlets* are shut out, and the trash left in. And besides that, we are likely to prove inhospitable to any new drama; since we are thinking in terms of past uses of the dramatic method as sanctioning any further use, we are likely to say that *Waiting for Godot* or *The Dumbwaiter* or *Zoo Story* is "not really a play," or that the playwrights "have evaded all the time-honored problems of the dramatist."

Suppose we refuse to commit that error, and think of drama as method rather than form. What, then, is that method? And what powers and limitations does it entail? The answer to the first question is apparently very simple. The dramatic method is one which presupposes representation by *enacting*. As far as enacting itself is concerned, it involves representation through the external behavior of the actors; as far as the audience is concerned, it involves the difference between witnessing something at first hand, seeing and hearing it for themselves, and having recounted to them, at second-hand, something which they have not witnessed. It involves, thus, the difference between their having something presented to them originally through their own senses of sight and hearing, and their having to make an imaginative construction of something out of materials supplied by someone else. So far so good; but what are the devices open to the actor? Here we must not become confused, as do so many authors of dramatic manuals, and say, "Why, voice, gesture, facial expression, etc." These are not the *devices* but the *materials* of representation. The devices of the actor are the *actual employments* of these. Reduced to general heads, they are very few. The actor can represent *directly*, either by *really* performing the act—say, walking or sitting down or kissing the heroine, or by *pretending* to perform it (you would have to have a new Romeo, Juliet, Tybalt, and Mercutio every night otherwise); or he can represent *indirectly*, by signs which imply certain things. Any possible external human action (waiving the limitations of a given theatre and the capacities of the actor) can be performed in reality; inconvenient and even certain impossible ones can be performed in pretense. But inner and private conditions, except when a character simply tells us what is happening inside him, can be set before us only indirectly, through certain outward signs from which we can infer them. Emotion, thought, moral habit, moral choice—these we must infer from signs. And there are basically two kinds of signs, natural and artificial. Weeping, laughing, groaning and the like are natural signs; they give us an outward effect from which we infer an inward cause; artificial signs depend not upon a cause-effect relation for their interpretation but upon some convention. Thus, in Nō drama the passing of the hand before the eyes is a sign of intense grief, and the spectator must know the convention in order to interpret.

Generally speaking, then, an action is dramatic to the extent that it may be conveyed by means of these devices; in a more restricted sense of the term "dramatic," to the extent that it is *more effective* when represented by these devices than it would be if conveyed by any other. And that is all there is. There are no rules or laws; there is no particular "dramatic form" as such; there is merely a certain body of devices, which can do certain things and cannot do certain others, which can do certain things better than, and other things less well than, other devices. *When* this body of devices is to be used, and *how*, and to *what extent*, and for *what end*, are questions we cannot answer by considering them in themselves, any more than we could by the simple scrutiny of a wheel or lever discover all of the uses to which wheel and lever may be put. Dramatic devices are conditions underlying the realization of *something further;* and we can discern whether they are well used, or whether they should have been used at all, only by consulting that something further. This is a matter of the various forms—the real *forms*—into which the dramatic method can enter. The moment we conceive of them we see that they are in fact quite numerous, and the short and dismal science of the theatre becomes a number of sciences, none of them short, and none of them dismal.

All of these forms, surely, present us with some kind of action. Nobody has as yet offered us a play in which the actors remain absolutely immobile, expressionless, and speechless for three acts; and no one ever will, except out of sheer ineptitude. All of them present us with action; but they differ very much in the kind of action they present, the purpose in presenting it, as well as in the materials and techniques which they use to present it. Some depict a serious, some a comic action; moreover, some do so for the sake of the action itself, as in the forms we call mimetic, some use the action as an instrument to prove a point, as in thesis plays and the forms we generally call didactic. Some seek to produce maximal excitement of certain emotions; others, like the Nō plays and like Sanskrit drama, to induce a serene contemplation. These actions may involve different principles of unity, although all seem to involve unity. The unity may be one of a train of consequences, as in *Hamlet;* or of relevance to a thesis, as in *Ghosts;* or of a group of characteristics amounting to a definition, as *Our Town* in a sense defines a certain kind of small-town life; or the unity may be that of a pattern, as in Schnitzler's *Reigen.* The actions may involve different kinds of probability: some, like realistic drama, employ a probability very close to natural probability; some, like fantasy, involve a probability deriving from a hypothesis *counter* to natural probability; others, like farce, entail a probability of exaggeration. The actions may differ in the number of incidents they involve; they may differ also in their manner of progression. Some move in a straight line;

some involve a turning-point; some are cyclical. They may involve a single line of action or several, and those with several lines may involve lines which are similar or contrasting in their emotional effect; they may involve, too, sub-plots as well as main plot, or simply coordinate lines of action. They may involve a single agent, with everyone else passive; or two or more agents, and these can be differently interrelated: the agents can be unwittingly operating at cross-purposes, or they can be in conflict. Finally—not that my account is exhaustive, but that a list must end somewhere—the action may stand for itself (compare so-called *literal representation* in painting and sculpture) or may mean more than itself, as in symbolic drama and allegory. The difference between Strindberg's *Miss Julie* and his *Spook Sonata* will illustrate my meaning.

So far we have merely been considering the different kinds of action which plays may have; but they differ also in their techniques of *representation;* that is, in their *scenarial* methods. The length of a play is a function not merely of the number of incidents but also of the scale on which they are represented. A full-length play, for instance, may consist of relatively few incidents depicted on a large scale, as in Racine's *Phèdre,* or it may consist of a great many incidents, some of which are depicted on a very small scale, as in *King Lear.* This difference of scale is among the most obvious ones of dramatic method, but it is by no means the only one. We are used to observing all kinds of *narrative* method: we know that the narrator may be an impersonal one, with theoretically unlimited knowledge of the action and agents (this is the author omniscient) or with definitely restricted knowledge (for instance, in Dashiell Hammett's *The Maltese Falcon* the narrator knows only the external behavior of his characters, whereas the narrator in Anais Nin's *Ladders of*

Fire often knows only the workings of their minds). Or the narrator can be a personal one, and he can be the principal agent, or someone close to or remote from the principal agent, and in the center or on the fringes of the action or outside it entirely, close to or remote from it in time; he can be good or bad, wise or foolish, hostile or friendly to the persons of the action, he can comment or not comment on the action; and there are many other possible differentiations. We should be unwise to suppose that whereas narrative offers such multiple possibilities, dramatic method is simple and uniform. For example, the dramatist may show his main action on the stage, as does Shakespeare, or he may have most of it happening off-stage, as does Chekhov. He may keep his main character in almost constant view, as Hamlet is kept, or never allow the character to appear, as with Anouilh's Ardèle. He may display chiefly physical actions, as in melodrama, or he may concentrate on the verbal actions, as in Racine's plays, or he may show his characters inside and out, as in *Strange Interlude*. He may let the events speak for themselves, or he may, as T. S. Eliot does, choose some character as his mouthpiece for comment, or he may like Aeschylus comment through a chorus. He may depict his characters and their actions in sharp circumstantial detail, like Shakespeare, or he may universalize them almost to the point of abstraction, like Racine. He may be bluntly explicit, or he may depend heavily upon suggestion and implication. He may present the events as happening at the moment, as is the usual way, or as being recollected, as in *The Glass Menagerie*. He can have the actors speak as well as act—again the usual way —or he can restrict them to pantomime while someone speaks for them, as in the old play of *Daniel*. And there are many other possibilities.

Dialogue, again, is no simple matter of high style or low

style, ornate or plain. It is governed by probabilities of character, thought, emotion, action, circumstance; it is governed, too, by the nature of the depiction as, for example, realistic or fantastic, as well as by convention, as well as by the kind of theatre for which it was intended. When the facilities of the theatre are few, and when the action requires sharp circumstantial detail, dramatic dialogue is likely to involve a great number of images, because the imagination of the audience must compensate for the shortcomings of stage representation; thus, Shakespearean dialogue is highly imagistic; notice, for example, the images which tell us of Elsinore or of the castle of Macbeth. When the possibilities of spectacle are great, dialogue tends to involve fewer images, as in the modern drama. What can be done by one means need not be done by another. Metaphor and simile too are no mere figures of speech in drama: there must always underlie in them the probability that the dramatic character would, just there and then *have seen* the similarity on which these depend; and his *seeing* that similarity must be significant. Dialogue may admit us to or exclude us from the innermost recesses of the human soul; it may fully express the inner workings, as in Shakespeare, or express them so little that they are unintelligible without stage directions, as in O'Neill.

For dialogue not only expresses thought, but also, through the forms and rhythms of speech, the passions and feelings of the character, through the signs of anger, pity, fear, and so on, which it affords. It does, indeed, a great deal more than that; for it constitutes all the *verbal* acts which the personages perform upon each—acts like commanding, informing, insulting, beseeching, threatening, deceiving—in short, all the things that people can do to each other by means of words. We do not merely *say* things, we *do* something by saying them.

The action (I use this term as including character and thought), the representation or scenario, and the dialogue make up the *general* parts of all plays; and there are no questions about plays *as plays* which do not refer to one or the other of them, and no dramatic analysis is complete without reference to *all* of them. Even if we do discuss all of them, however, our analysis is not necessarily complete; for a play is a whole, and unless we discuss these parts as functioning within that whole, we shall not be discussing them as *parts* but merely as *topics*. We must not do, therefore, as Addison does in his *Spectator* papers on *Paradise Lost;* for though he discusses the plot, character, thought, and diction of the epic, he does so as if they were entirely independent things, referring each to separate external, and indeed unrelated, criteria. We must rather discover how part subserves part to constitute a whole.

As we work thus through play after play, we shall find that the forms and devices of drama are far more various than we had supposed. We shall learn, too, to distrust the easy labels which inertia or ignorance impose so readily, and the rigid formulas which do not work. We shall come, thus, to a better understanding not only of what drama has been in the past but also of what it is now and what it may be in the future; and, in the discovery of the true principles of drama, make dramatic theory commensurate with dramatic art, and learn what it means to approach a play *as a play*.

Notes

CHAPTER I

1. Reprinted in Paul Lauter, *Theories of Comedy* (New York: Doubleday, 1964 [Anchor Book A 403]), pp. 432-43.
2. L. J. Potts, *Comedy* (London, 1949), p. 15.
3. *Philebus* 48 C.
4. Cicero, *De Oratore*, II. lviii.
5. *Laughter,* ch. 1, sec. v.
6. *Leviathan,* Part I, ch. vi.
7. *Critique of Aesthetic Judgment*, Book II, sec. 54.
8. *The World as Will and Idea*, Vol. I, sec. 13.
9. "On the Essence of Laughter," in *The Mirror of Art*, translated and edited by Jonathan Mayne (New York: Doubleday, 1956), p. 131 ff.
10. *The English Comic Writers*, Lecture I.
11. *Jokes and Their Relation to the Unconscious*, ch. vii.
12. *Introduction to Aesthetics*, sec. 28.
13. *The Foundation of Aesthetics*, Part VI, ch. vii.

CHAPTER IV

1. *Greek Comedy* (New York: Hill and Wang [Dramabook Edition], 1963), p. 299.
2. *Plautus: The Rope and Other Plays*, translated by E. F. Watling (Baltimore: Penguin Books Ltd., 1964), pp. 12-13.

CHAPTER V

1. *La Critique de l'Ecole des Femmes,* sc. i. (My translations throughout this chapter.)
2. *Le Tartuffe,* Act I, sc. vi.
3. *Molière et la Comédie,* viii.
4. *Le Tartuffe,* Act III, sc. ii.
5. *L'Avare,* Act V, sc. ii.

INDEX

(Main references exclusive of the Appendix)